ELVIS PRESLEY

ROBERT LOVE

ELVIS PRESLEY

FRANKLIN WATTS
NEW YORK I LONDON I TORONTO I SYDNEY I 1986
AN IMPACT BIOGRAPHY

Photographs courtesy of:
Movie Star News: pp. 8, 30, 49, 91, 120;
Florida Times-Union, May 12, 1955: p. 11;
AP/Wide World: pp. 18, 56, 72, 77;
UPI/Bettmann Newsphotos: pp. 20, 70,
74, 75, 81, 82, 100, 104, 107, 112;
Globe Photos: p. 23;
Michael Ochs Archives: pp. 43, 46;
RCA Records: p. 63;
Movie Still Archives: p. 78.

Library of Congress Cataloging in Publication Data

Love, Robert, 1951–
Elvis Presley.

(An Impact biography)
Bibliography: p.
Includes index.
Summary: Follows the life, career, and music of the
influential and popular rock and roll star, from his
early years in Mississippi to his controversial death.
1. Presley, Elvis, 1935–77—Juvenile literature.
2. Singers—United States—Biography—Juvenile
literature. [1. Presley, Elvis, 1935–77. 2. Singers.
3. Rock music] I. Title.
ML3930.P73L7 1986 784.5′4′00924 [B] [92] 86-5656
ISBN 0-531-10239-4

CONTENTS

INTRODUCTION

On May 12, 1955, Elvis Presley arrived in Jacksonville, Florida, at the wheel of a brand-new pink Cadillac. Six months before, he had been driving a truck for Crown Electric in his hometown of Memphis, Tennessee, and taking a lot of ribbing for his flashy clothes and long sideburns. Since then he had made three records that sold pretty well in some parts of the South, but not one had made the national charts. In fact, here in Florida, not very many people knew who he was.

That night, he would perform before 14,000 people at the local ball park—as an opening act in a traveling country and western show. Elvis would go on just before intermission, a spot given to him for a very good reason: he was an impossible act to follow. The other performers had seen what he could do to a crowd. He whipped them up as a preacher would, but it wasn't religion he was preaching. The young teenagers, especially the girls, screamed and cried throughout his songs, and even carried on after he left the stage

But the Jacksonville audience didn't know that yet. They had come to see and hear the headliner, Hank Snow, and the other well-known acts in this jamboree, such as the Carter Sisters and Slim Whitman, who would appear in the second half of the show. In fact, it's likely that few in the crowd had even heard of this twenty-year-old singer with the odd name, Elvis Presley, the Hillbilly Cat.

At 9 P.M., the sky was dark, and Elvis bolted onto the middle of the stage wearing a pink suit with flowing pink pants pegged tight at the ankles and a lacy white shirt. With his hair slicked back on the sides and tumbling down in front of his face, he fixed a defiant, sultry glare at the first few rows. Then, bam!, without an introduction, without even a warning, Elvis and his little band kicked into their first song with a vengeance.

He threw his hips into songs such as "That's All Right, Mama." He bent the microphone down as if it were a lover for "Baby, Let's Play House." He jumped, he bopped, he twitched like a man possessed by the rhythm, pounding his guitar as much as playing it. The audience was stunned.

It sounded something like "Negro" music, but the singer was this incredibly handsome white boy with pomaded hair and a winsome hillbilly twang. To the parents and grandparents in the audience he must have seemed a strange and discomforting figure. But it wasn't long before the teenagers, even those who hadn't heard the news yet, realized that this wasn't music for the family. This music was for them! Before anyone knew it, the screams of teenage girls—hundreds of them—rose up and started to drown out the music.

Well, all right! Just as it had happened in Texas and Tennessee, tonight the screams came right on cue. Now Elvis took control. As the Blue Moon Boys rocked through tune after tune, Elvis teased the audience. He made the screams go louder with an insinuating twitch of his hips. He'd stare at a girl in the front row and her eyes would turn up in ecstasy. He had perfected this routine in high school auditoriums all over the South. After the last song, dripping with sweat, Elvis thanked the audience. He called them "ladies and gentlemen." Then, addressing the part of his audience that he best knew how to handle, he lowered his voice and whispered into the mike. "Girls, I'll see you backstage."

On May 12, 1955, the Florida Times-Union carried an advertisement for Hank Snow's All Star Jamboree. Among the performers was one unknown to the local audience—Elvis Presley, appearing with "Bill and Scotty" (Bill Black and Scotty Moore). Elvis's performance that night marked a turning point in his career.

Suddenly all hell broke loose. The audience started rushing the stage. The Jacksonville police, who had never seen anything like this at a country music jamboree before, did their best to keep him safe, but with little success. Elvis's new fans chased him all the way to the dugout that led to the performer's dressing room. Elvis breathed a sigh of relief, but a moment later the door burst open and he was swamped again. Some fool had forgotten to lock the door.

A wave of southern femininity—more than a hundred die-hards in bobby sox and frilly blouses—cornered their new-found hero. They attacked him, ripping off his clothes and his shoes, still screaming madly. To escape, Elvis climbed atop a shower stall while the police cleared the room. When the last overheated teenage girl was escorted outside, and it was safe to go out, Elvis walked up to the brand-new pink Cadillac that his early success had financed. He found it covered from fin to bumper with girls' names—scrawled in lipstick and nail polish, scratched into the car's paint with pins and rings and ballpoint pens. Surveying the damaged symbol of his youthful success, Elvis must have smiled. He didn't care. By this time, he knew there would be plenty of other Cadillacs.

The Jacksonville newspapers accurately described what happened the night before as a "riot," but the reporters couldn't have known that they had also witnessed the start of a revolution. A shy, self-effacing truck driver from Memphis had made Jacksonville, Florida, a stopover on his way to becoming the King of rock and roll. Jacksonville—and America—would never be the same.

Within a year, teenagers all over America would be in a fever for rock and roll, and Elvis was the one who served it up with all the trimmings. Elvis not only sang like nobody had ever heard before, but he danced like a man on fire to the new beat. And he looked really *COOL!* If adults wanted to know the attraction, kids were likely to say, "Elvis is crazy, man; he's really gone." The girls would squeal hysterically. If mom and dad didn't get it, who cared? He belonged to the kids.

In so many ways, Elvis was different from the bland music of the Hit Parade. Those were songs your parents could listen to. Elvis's songs spoke honestly about feelings that teenagers were feeling. He became a sensation and a hero overnight. In the wake of his success, parts of the country tried to outlaw Elvis and those who followed in his path. They called rock and roll the devil's music and tried to stamp it out, but all they really did was fan the flames.

Almost a decade after he died, Elvis's popularity continues to thrive. Each new generation seems to discover in him part of themselves. To date, Elvis has sold more records than any other single performer in the history of recorded music. He made thirty-one movies, and played live for millions of fans. His fame was so widespread that at one point in his life, a Gallup poll determined that his was the most recognized name in the world.

But Elvis Presley's greatest contribution cannot be measured by record sales or box office receipts. He changed the landscape of American music and popular culture. In a part of the country where racial segregation was the rule, Elvis dared to fuse black music with white. Such an act—at once defiant, bold, and even dangerous—produced a new style of music that eventually became a permanent and distinctively American form: rock and roll.

For this daring, he was alternately loved and condemned, idolized and threatened. Finally, Elvis rose to a level of fame and worship that few ever know and even fewer survive.

Elvis became a mythic American figure, like Paul Bunyan and John Henry, men of legendary strength and stamina. But Elvis was not just a legend. As a human being, he possessed the usual abundance of contradictions and weaknesses.

Though he saw himself primarily as an entertainer in the mold of Frank Sinatra and Dean Martin, his creative spirit changed the course of popular culture. His very image defined for parents of the 1950s the danger of teenage rebellion, but he devoted himself to his parents, and remained polite and deferential to his elders. He took the natural expression of his youthful passion and exuberance and perfected it into calculated stage tricks to keep his audience on the edge of frenzy. Yet his every move seemed spontaneous and natural. He hated drug abusers but he abused prescription medicines until he finally killed himself. Finally, he gave his talent and his energy until there was no more to give. For that, at the least, we should remember and honor him.

THE
SURVNING
SON

1

On the bitter cold night of January 8, 1935, in northern Mississippi, the pains of labor meant the end of a difficult pregnancy for twenty-two-year-old Gladys Love Presley. She told her neighbors early on that she would deliver twins—twin boys, in fact—she was sure of it. And she was right.

At 4 A.M., Elvis's twin brother, Jesse Garon, was delivered stillborn. Sorrow instead of joy settled on the ramshackle little house on North Saltillo Road, in East Tupelo, Mississippi. Thirty-five minutes later, Elvis Aron was born.

Jesse Garon was laid out in a tiny cardboard coffin in the front room and buried the next day in an unmarked grave in nearby Priceville Cemetery. Gladys was devastated by the death of her first-born son. Her grief seemed to be unending; not long after, she told everyone that she would not be able to bear any more children.

When Elvis grew a little older, Gladys would take him to Jesse's grave. There, she told him that he could talk to his twin brother through prayer. She spoke Jesse's name constantly, always referring to him in the present tense as if he were alive. To the young Elvis, it must have seemed that his brother was as alive as he was. This sense of spirituality and otherworldliness was passed on to Elvis from both his parents, and it never left him.

One block from the Presley home, the First Assembly of God Church occupied a modest one-story frame house, not

This two-room frame house in East Tupelo,
Mississippi, was the birthplace of Elvis
Presley in 1935. Restored to what it might
have looked like when Elvis was born, it
is now a tourist attraction.

unlike the cabins and bungalows around it. East Tupelo was a dirt-poor town, and the Presleys were about as poor as a family could get without being destitute. In the nearby town of Tupelo, the population of six thousand was still in the depths of the Great Depression. Opportunities to make a decent living were few and far between.

Elvis's parents were the children of sharecroppers, farmers who were so poor they didn't own the land they farmed. Gladys had to quit working as a sewing-machine operator when she became pregnant, and Elvis's father, Vernon, who had drifted from job to job, began working for a dairy, delivering milk from house to house. To build their 30-by-15-foot (914 x 457 cm), two-room cabin, Vernon had to borrow money from his boss. He was probably making less than fifteen dollars a week. He could not afford to pay the fifteen-dollar fee to the doctor who delivered Elvis.

THE CHURCH'S INFLUENCE

Despite their financial worries, the family found sustenance in religion. Every Sunday, the Presleys attended the 11 A.M. service at the First Assembly of God Church along with the other two dozen members of the congregation. The First Assembly, somtimes called Holy Rollers, taught a strict interpretation of the Bible—including a vision of hell as a place of fire and brimstone. As a Fundamentalist Christian sect, it banned tobacco and alcohol, and forbade dances and movies. Music was allowed, but only if it was performed in the service of the Lord.

It was here that the young Elvis first heard gospel music, singing with his family and the congregation hymns such as "I'll Fly Away" and "When the Roll Is Called Up Yonder." Though the First Assembly's services were sedate compared to those of the neighboring black churches, the music made Elvis so excited that he couldn't sit still. People who remem-

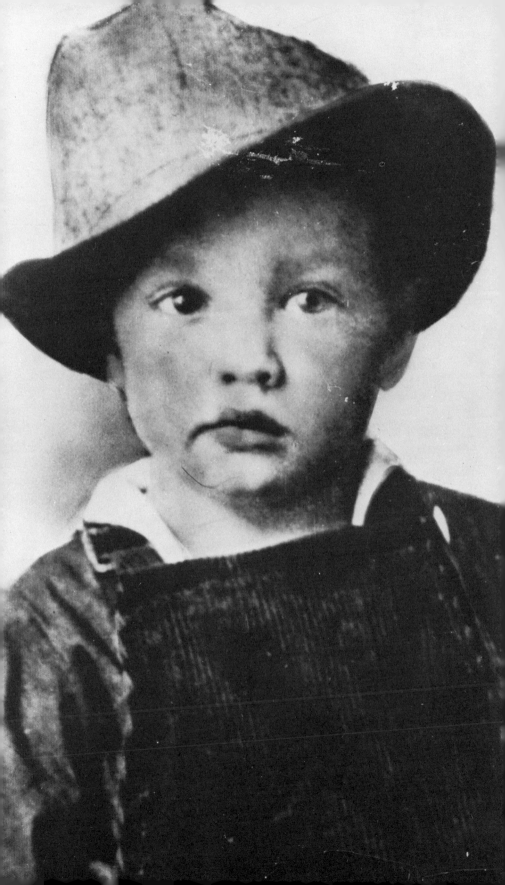

ber him as a little boy recall that he always managed to squirm away from his parents during the service to stand up with the choir.

With his parents Elvis also attended the religious camp meetings and revivals that were then popular in the South. At these meetings a wide-eyed Elvis witnessed not only the professional singing gospel groups but also the flamboyant preachers who could really fire up a crowd. Later on it became obvious that the young Elvis had been not only a watcher but a learner as well. Years later, when asked about the origins of his famous gyrating stage movements, Elvis said, "There were these singers, perfectly fine singers, but nobody responded to them. Then, there was the preachers, and they cut up all over the place, jumpin' on the piano, movin' ever' which way. The audience liked 'em."

HARD TIMES

Elvis's home life, however, was anything but wild. His parents impressed upon him at an early age the courtly Southern manners that he retained even in his days as a superstar. He always answered "Yes, sir," "ma'am," and said "please." He stood out of respect when a person older than himself entered the room, and he spoke only when he was spoken to.

These were the rules, according to Elvis's parents, that helped a young man "get along in the world." As Gladys and Vernon Presley had learned firsthand, life could be a bitter

Elvis at age 3. His twin brother, Jesse, had died at birth.

struggle, full of disappointments, and the family had seen their share. Not long after Jesse Garon died, Gladys's mother fell ill and died a lingering death from tuberculosis. Her father had died only the year before.

Vernon Presley, never an ambitious man, now had a child and a wife to support. When Elvis was still a little boy, Vernon foolishly forged a check made out to his employer, and was caught. He was sentenced to three years in a notoriously brutal labor camp called Parchman. After he was taken away, Gladys lost the family's house and she had to move into the house next door with Vernon's parents. Now she had to go back to work, taking in sewing and laundry. Her only son consumed her few spare moments.

The neighbors would always say that Gladys never let Elvis out of her sight, even for a minute. When Elvis turned five, she began walking him to school, a morning ritual that didn't stop until his senior year in high school. Gladys always feared that something terrible would happen to her son if she wasn't vigilant. Elvis himself had terrible fears—reflected in his nightmares—that his father would again be taken from him—this time forever. In reality, Vernon spent very little time at home until Elvis was eleven. Even when Vernon was released from prison in 1941, he headed north to Memphis, where he found work in a defense plant. The job took him about a hundred miles away, so he returned to his family only on the weekends.

Family photographs from Elvis's boyhood years reveal the toll that life had taken on the young family. Vernon's jaw

Elvis with his parents in 1941, soon after Vernon Presley was released from prison.

is set and his eyes stare at the camera, defiant and proud. Gladys casts her glance downward. She looks worried. No one in the family is smiling. Their hope for a little security and an escape from the hardscrabble existence of their first twenty years had so far been unfulfilled. But these hopes, naturally, were transferred to their young son.

THE
GROWING-UP
YEARS

2

Elvis's first "break" came when he was ten years old. In the fifth grade at the time, he sang a song called "Old Shep" for his teacher. She was so impressed that she took him to the principal and made him sing it again. The principal, equally impressed, took Elvis to the Mississippi-Alabama Fair and Dairy Show to compete in the local talent contest. Without accompaniment, and standing on a chair to reach the microphone, Elvis sang the song—which laments the loss of a favorite dog. He surprised even himself by winning second prize—five dollars and free rides at the amusement park all day.

Prize or no prize, Elvis was still a normal ten-year-old boy who cared a lot more for other things besides singing. For his eleventh birthday, Elvis wanted a bicycle or a rifle. His mother had something else in mind though, as she took him down to the Tupelo Hardware Company in January of 1946.

The owner of the store, a man named Forrest Bobo, remembers that when Gladys told Elvis that he couldn't have the .22 caliber rifle that he wanted, he threw a temper tantrum. After a few minutes of quiet discussion, the storeowner and Gladys persuaded Elvis to accept a guitar. The store had three models, one that cost $3.50, one for $6.25, and one for $12.50. Although the family was poor, Gladys got him the most expensive guitar in the store.

His uncles Vester and Johnny taught him a few chords, and Elvis began trying to imitate the singers he heard on the radio. At night, he listened to country and western music broadcast from places far away from East Tupelo, big cities such as Nashville and Memphis, Tennessee. To him, these places must have seemed as far away as the Orient, and equally as mysterious and alluring.

In 1946, the family moved into town. Vernon had found work driving a truck for a Tupelo grocery firm. They moved to a series of small apartments in the city's slums. While attending junior high school, Elvis met the brother of Mississippi Slim, who was Tupelo's resident country and western performer. Mississippi Slim had a live radio show every Saturday morning on WELO, and Elvis visited the radio station as often as he could, soaking up the atmosphere, and seeing with his own eyes what he had only listened to before.

Two years later, when Elvis was thirteen, the Presleys moved again—this time abruptly—to an even bigger city, Memphis. It's possible that Vernon had gotten himself into trouble again, but one thing was certain. "We were broke, man, broke, and we left Tupelo overnight," Elvis said later. "We just headed to Memphis. Things had to be better."

Elvis entered L.C. Humes High School, a technical and vocational school, after the school year had begun. He was painfully self-conscious, a country boy lost in the big city. Just the size of his new school overwhelmed him. Humes had sixteen-hundred students—more students than the entire population of East Tupelo. He must have been shy; not one of his classmates during his first two years there had any recollection of him.

Elvis didn't stand out in any way at this time of his life. He was an average student academically. Much of his time was spent in shop class, but he did a little bit better in the subject he liked—English. While keeping to himself at school, Elvis continued to sing and play the guitar at home, often performing for friends and family on the steps outside the Lauderdale Courts, the public housing projects where the family now lived. He was still so unsure of himself, however, that he often waited until dark before he began to play. And when he did, his favorite songs were sentimental country and western ballads of the type Eddy Arnold sang.

IN HIS OWN IMAGE

After he turned sixteen, Elvis became obsessed about his physical appearance, especially about his hair and clothes. He had arrived in Memphis as a farm boy in overalls. Now he began making himself over in the image of the slick city rebel. After several experiments with his hair, including a Mohawk and a disastrous home perm, Elvis chose the hairstyle of one of his favorite movie actors, Tony Curtis. His locks were now swept back from both sides into a high crown and waxed to gleaming perfection with Royal Crown Pomade, a thick grease used by Memphis blacks. His trademark sideburns were also growing in.

He began to shop at Lansky Brothers, a Beale Street store favored by sharp-dressing hipsters, hustlers, and musicians. Down on Beale Street the look of the day was iridescent and loud, and to the poor teenager from Tupelo, it no doubt seemed the height of urban sophistication. A typical Lansky Brothers outfit consisted of gabardine trousers pegged tight at the ankles, billowing upward and bundled at the waistband in a series of sharp pleats. Lightning bolt motifs were very popular. So were shirts in lime green and shocking pink with elaborate rolled collars turned straight up for maximum effect. Finish it off with shiny white shoes.

An outfit like that was just the beginning of what would eventually become Elvis's image. Elvis pieced together his look from a variety of sources: the local Memphis sharpies, the country and western and gospel singers he saw occa-

sionally, and, most important, the movies. Elvis loved the movies, and spent much of his free time in this traditional refuge of the lonely teenager. During the years as an outsider, he not only took comfort from them, but built his fantasy image of himself around his screen heroes, most notably Tony Curtis.

In *City Across the River* and several films in the early 1950s Curtis portrayed an alienated young tough, sensitive, misunderstood—a character with much in common with the way Elvis and many other teenage boys saw themselves. Elvis carefully copied Curtis's look, his stance, and even the spit curl dangling in front of his face. He perfected the image in the summer of 1951, and took it with him when he went back to school in the fall.

To say that his new image did not go over in working-class Humes High would be an understatement. Elvis was still the same shy self-effacing boy of the year before, but his new appearance made him stick out like a sore thumb. Crewcuts were the order of the day, and a boy's hair that was longer than that was considered too effeminate and weird. Not only did Elvis wear his hair long, he spent countless hours at the mirror, trying to get it just right. It was an invitation to a lynching—his own.

Red West, a high-school friend who later became one of Elvis's bodyguards, remembered what Elvis was like in his book, *Elvis: What Happened?* "Someone was always picking on him. . . . It was that hair, man—it got him into all kinds of trouble. If he had a regular haircut like the rest of us, he prob-

Elvis giving it his all.
This photo was probably
taken in 1956.

ably wouldn't have been bothered. But I guess the other kids thought he was trying to show off or something."

Elvis might have looked different to his classmates, but he wanted to fit in. He went out for the football team in the eleventh grade and made it, but lasted on the squad only a few weeks because he refused to cut his hair. Red West, a year younger than Elvis but big and burly even in his teens, recalls encountering him in the boys' room. Elvis had been pinned to the wall by a group of rowdy teammates who were about to give him a haircut by force. "He was looking like a frightened little animal and I just couldn't stand seeing it," Red remembers. "When you're very poor, you tend to let everyone look after their own troubles, but that face of Elvis's, I can still see it to this day. . . . It's a child's face, and it asks for help."

Red rescued Elvis that day, as he had done once before when Elvis was threatened by a group of bullies out in front of the school. Elvis never forgot these incidents, according to Red.

Although the sixteen-year-old Elvis had donned the clothes of defiance and rebellion (in fact he defined the image of the juvenile delinquent later on), he was still a frightened young boy who wanted to join in. Not only did he join the football team—even with his greasy pompadour—but he also joined the high school's ROTC chapter and posed proudly for his picture in uniform. He even told friends that his life's ambition was to become a Tennessee State Highway patrolman.

The image might have been shaky, but Elvis had started to conquer his fears of singing in front of strangers. His history teacher, Mildred Scrivener, cajoled him into entering the school's variety show. Out of thirty acts, the one that got the most applause would get to do an encore at the end of the show.

Dressed in a borrowed red shirt, Elvis sang "Old Shep," the ballad that had won him second prize seven years before at the Mississippi-Alabama state fair. It worked even better for him this time; by the end of the show, no one in the auditorium doubted that he had gotten the most applause. But Elvis, shy as ever, hid at the side of the stage and practically had to be pushed back out for his encore. "I'll never forget the look on his face when he came off the stage from doing the encore," his teacher remembered. "They really liked me, Miss Scrivener," he said. "They really liked me."

The rest of high school passed uneventfully for Elvis. He behaved pretty much like the rest of the kids. He went to parties, to hayrides, and, as always, to the movies at the Suzore Theater in downtown Memphis. He dated a few girls and occasionally entertained at gatherings with a little more confidence. He left only the slightest impression on those around him, preferring the quiet of his own thoughts and fantasies. At the same time, though, he continued to listen and watch intently, to absorb the influences that would shape his musical career.

THE GOSPEL
MUSIC INFLUENCE

When he was sixteen, Elvis attended his first "all-night sing," a once-a-month late-night showcase for the great white gospel groups of the South. A crowd of several thousand people would gather to see and hear four or five of the gospel quartets perform. And perform they did. Dressed in sharp, flashy stage clothes and wild hairstyles, moving with precision steps, and singing sophisticated harmonies, these performers worked their magic on the crowd—and on Elvis. Never had the music of the Lord moved the way it did when these boys leaned into the mikes and let go. This was ol' time religion with sequins, barbershop harmonies with bounce—in short, a full-fledged show based around the songs that Elvis had heard performed only by choirs. He returned to the showcase time after time.

The late-night gospel sings at Ellis Auditorium were hosted by the Blackwood Brothers, a popular quartet made up of members of the First Assembly of God—Elvis's church. In fact one of the younger members of the family attended Sunday school with Elvis, and brought him backstage to meet his relatives. Elvis soon became such a constant presence that the only time he wasn't there was when he couldn't afford to go, a problem he quickly solved by selling soft drinks during intermission. Backstage at Ellis Auditorium, Elvis met some of the men who would permanently influence his musical style.

The most flamboyant of these professional gospel singers was Jake Hess, lead singer of the Statesmen. Jake had a great booming voice and a unique vocal style: he would slice the words of a lyric into rhythmic punches, accentuating each syllable. The crowds really loved him.

Elsewhere in Memphis, black gospel music had evolved into a much different style. This was a less polished, but more urgent and emotional kind of gospel music that Elvis heard on the radio. It's not known whether the shy young teenager made frequent trips to hear the black gospel singers or to Beale Street, known as the home of the blues. What we do know from him was that he listened to music like this on records and the radio as much as he could.

Memphis's black radio station, WDIA, sent out a steady stream of blues, gospel, and R&B, along with religious inspiration delivered by fast-talking disk jockeys. Elvis has said that he listened to the station constantly, and there is every reason to believe that much of his education about black music and style came from this station.

The "Mother Station of the Negroes," as WDIA was called, familiarized Elvis with the full range of black music, both religious and secular, as well as a black sensibility. The black DJs passed along the patter of the street, along with jokes and religious sermons, not to mention the latest rhythm and blues records.

For the five years that Elvis spent in Memphis before becoming a professional singer, WDIA went on the air every day and later became a very powerful station. It helped popularize the musical style of R&B, a fusing of the country blues with a heavy, driving beat. This type of music, which was also very influential in Elvis's musical career, came out of the black ghettos in the years after World War II. Its popularity grew among whites largely due to radio. Elvis realized the debt he owed to black R&B artists such as Clyde McPhatter and Big Joe Turner. When he became successful, Elvis tried to pay back some of this musical debt by donating money to WDIA.

When he wasn't listening to the radio, Elvis listened to records. With a date, Elvis would sometimes go to one of his favorite haunts, Charlie's record shop, across the street from the movie theater. There, at Elvis's insistence, they would listen to the latest blues records over Coca-Colas. He was knowledgeable about the latest releases, whether they were blues or gospel, black or white. Though his lackluster high-school education was near completion, Elvis's musical education now went into high gear.

THE WORKING MAN

Elvis graduated from Humes High in 1953. His yearbook photo shows him in a dark suit and solid colored tie, his face marred by acne, and his hair piled into a greasy swirl high on his head. A little spit curl hangs over his forehead. Only a few years later, Elvis Presley would be known as a world-famous teenage heartthrob, but it's hard to imagine this from his yearbook picture.

Without his dreams and his ambition what awaited Elvis was the same future that faced many of his blue-collar classmates: manual labor at hourly wages. As a high school graduate, Elvis had no marketable skills and very few academic accomplishments to his credit. With no other choice, Elvis followed the example of his uncles, Travis and Johnny, and went to work at the Precision Tool Company. For $1.65 an hour, Elvis and his cousin Gene Smith toiled on an assembly line putting together shell casings for the army. Not only was the work tedious, but the two teenagers spent much of their time fending off the barbs and insults directed at them for their long hair.

A few months later Elvis quit to become a truck driver for the Crown Electric Company. The pay wasn't as good—$41 a week instead of the $65 he had averaged on the assembly line—but the freedom of the road appealed to him. He would drive his Ford pickup full of materials to the various construction sites around town. Along the way, he saw a lot of Memphis, and no doubt he slowed down more than once in front of 706 Union Avenue, home of the Memphis Recording Service. There would come a day when he would not only slow down but park the pickup and go inside.

ROCK
AND
ROLL
IS BORN

3

"We Record Anything—Anywhere—Anytime." That was the advertising claim of the Memphis Recording Service. Sam Phillips, a former disc jockey, ran the studio as a part-time business. He also worked as the recording engineer for a local Memphis radio station. Aside from recording weddings, speeches, or funerals for nine dollars per side, Sam turned on the tape recorder for anyone who walked in and wanted to cut a 78-rpm record. It cost four dollars.

Sam also acted as a kind of talent scout for local musicians, recording demonstration records of regional performers and sending them off to record companies in the big cities. If the song sold enough copies, Sam received a few cents per record.

His own preference was for "race records," rhythm-and-blues tunes recorded by black artists who he felt were more vital than the popular white singers and country performers. Sam later explained, "It seemed to me that the Negroes were the only ones who had any freshness left in their music." Some moderate successes with records by Bobby "Blue" Bland, Chester "Howlin' Wolf" Burnett, and Ike Turner (whose former wife is the pop singer Tina Turner) convinced Phillips to go into business for himself as an independent record producer.

It was at this point, in the fall of 1953, that the future King of rock and roll—on his lunch hour—stopped his truck in front of 706 Union Avenue and spent four dollars of his hard-earned money just to hear what his voice sounded like.

THE FIRST RECORD

Sam Phillips was out of the studio at the time, but his assistant and secretary, Marion Keisker, led Elvis into the recording studio. When Marion asked who he sounded like, Elvis shot back, "I don't sound like anyone." The two songs he chose to record were by the Ink Spots, a popular black trio. When Marion played the tape back to press the record, she decided to make a copy for Sam to hear. Something in Elvis's high, plaintive voice reminded her of what Sam always said. "If I could find a white boy who had the Negro sound and the Negro feel, I could make a billion dollars." She wrote down Elvis's phone number and his address on Alabama Street, and remembers remarking to herself that "the kid with the sideburns" has some talent.

Sam listened to the recording and agreed that "the kid" had a good voice. Nevertheless, he told Marion that Elvis wasn't ready for a recording career yet. She pestered Sam many times over the next few months to give Elvis a chance, but nothing ever came of it until about nine months later. A demonstration record arrived, by an unidentified young black man with a high sweet voice. The song, "Without You," had commercial potential, but the singer was just an unknown amateur, and black at that. For a record to become a national hit at that time, Sam knew, the singer had to be white.

One more time, Marion suggested that Elvis be given a try, and Sam relented. Marion called the Presley home on a Saturday afternoon. Naturally, Elvis was at the movies, but Gladys said she would go and get him. Elvis was obviously excited, Marion remembers, because when he arrived, "I was still standing there with the telephone in my hand, and here comes Elvis, panting. I think he ran all the way."

Elvis's first try at "Without You" was a disaster. Try as he might, Elvis couldn't master the sophisticated ballad. There was a second and a third take, without much improvement. Obviously frustrated, Sam shouted, "Well, what can you do?"

Almost immediately, Elvis launched into a manic medley of bits and pieces of various songs. It was as if all the music he had absorbed since he was a boy was trying to get out at the same time. He literally banged on his guitar. He sang gospel tunes, country and western, even some songs by his current favorite, Dean Martin. Nothing Sam heard that day convinced him that the kid with the sideburns was ready for a recording career. Sam recommended more practice; Elvis said what he needed was a band.

It was probably kindness on Sam's part that made him call an ambitious twenty-one-year-old guitar player named Scotty Moore. Scotty had a job at his brother's dry-cleaning plant, but he wanted to break into the music business. Scotty and Elvis got together and during a rehearsal were joined by Bill Black, who played bass with Scotty in a band that played "hillbilly" music.

Sam offered them the use of the Sun studios as an after-hours rehearsal hall for the next few months. Marion recalls that they worked mainly on "developing a style." Though no one in the trio knew exactly what that style would be, it's obvious now what they were seeking: an integration of white country music and black rhythm and blues—the revved-up form of music that Sam thought would make him a billion dollars.

A few months later, on July 6, 1954, Sam let the tape recorders roll. Elvis's first professional recording session, like his first amateur attempt, started rather badly. The first number they tried, a sentimental country ballad called "I Love You Because," even had a spoken recitation in the middle of it. It was corny. Sam was not impressed.

They went through a few more country and western songs, but nothing special was happening. After a while Scotty and Bill took a break. They sat there drinking Cokes, while Sam did paperwork in the control room. Then Elvis began having a little fun with a blues song called "That's All Right, Mama." Probably to let off a little steam, Elvis started jumping around, beating on his guitar, trying to get the guys to laugh. Scotty found the key and laid in some lead guitar. Then Bill started thumping on the bass, and what followed was a joyful and spontaneous sendup of Arthur "Big Boy" Crudup's 1947 electric blues. To the boys, it was a joke. That was black music they were playing, not something that would make a hit record.

Suddenly, Sam came running out of the control booth and demanded, "What in the devil are you doing?" Elvis responded, "I don't know, just goofing off." Sam told them to figure it out quick before they lost it, and headed back to the control booth to get it down on tape. This was more like what he wanted. The record was finished on the third or fourth take.

A NEW KIND OF SOUND

"That's All Right, Mama" was the sound that Sam Phillips had in mind all along, and he knew it. It was a blues tune put through the paces, set to a galloping country rhythm. At the same time, though, Elvis's vocal kept the essential blues feel. Suddenly—and much to his surprise—Elvis was in his element. This was the kind of music Elvis liked to listen to. Actually, it was *two* kinds of music that Elvis liked. He had

Elvis, dressed for success

simply combined them as a joke, and what do you know, Sam had gone running for the tape recorder.

Encouraged by Sam Phillips's fatherly approval, Elvis began playing with the tune, testing the range of his high, youthful voice. He let the words and melody ride the rhythm, sliding and swooping from note to note on the chorus. The result was an insinuating vocal with impeccable timing.

In Scotty Moore's recollection, the trio spent three or four more nights trying to come up with the "B" side to "That's All Right." It wasn't until Bill Black started clowning around on a bluegrass standard called "Blue Moon of Kentucky" that the second moment of magic happened. This time it was Bill Black cutting loose, mimicking the pure, high falsetto of sing-er Bill Monroe. Scotty and Elvis chimed in with the rhythm. Then, Elvis took the melody down to his range, tinged it with some blue notes and swooping glissandos and, in Scotty Moore's words, "That was the first record."

The style of these recordings on Sun Records would later be called "rockabilly," but in 1954, the sound was unknown and unnamed. Actually, the style just tumbled from three young guys making fun of songs they knew well. When Elvis treated songs with respect, or tried to imitate the singers who sang them, he got nowhere. When he and Scotty and Bill relaxed, they took the songs and made them over again as something new. "Unique," Sam called it.

Because this first record was a true fusion of black and white styles, the three musicians and Sam Phillips agreed that it was exciting—and potentially dangerous. At the time, whites in the South, which was still rigidly segregated, didn't look favorably upon anyone who mixed with blacks, even musically. While Sam might have been happy with a little controversy to stir up record sales, Scotty Moore predicted, "They'll run us out of town."

Sam liked what the boys had done, but he had no idea how to peddle it. His best bet was a white disc jockey named

Dewey Phillips (no relation), a fast-talking hillbilly hepcat whose "Red Hot and Blue" radio show on Memphis station WHBQ featured only black music. Dewey had premiered other Sun records, but he wasn't sure about this one—after all, Sam had already told him that the singer was a white kid.

Elvis tuned in the family radio to WHBQ for Vernon and Gladys and lit out for his favorite hiding place, the movies. He might have been shy and nervous about hearing himself on the radio, but he also must have feared public humiliation for trying to sound like "a Negro." When "That's All Right" went out over the Memphis airwaves, Dewey Phillips's phone lines lit up and stayed lit the rest of the night. There were so many requests, that starting about nine-thirty, he just continued to play the record, first one side and then the other, over and over again. Dewey decided that, with this overwhelming response to the record, he better get "the kid with the sideburns" down to the station for an interview.

Once again Gladys, this time accompanied by her husband, went to find Elvis in the protective darkness of the movie theater. When Elvis saw them coming down the aisle, he whispered, "What's happening, Momma?"

Gladys replied, "Plenty, son, but it's all good."

At the radio station, a nervous and out-of-breath Elvis confessed to Dewey Phillips that he "didn't know nuthin 'bout bein' interviewed." Dewey told him, "Just don't say nuthin' dirty." The disc jockey wanted to make sure that the listeners knew this singer with the black sound was white, so he asked Elvis where he went to high school. Everyone in Memphis knew that L. C. Humes was an all-white school.

Sun Records received orders for six-thousand records within days of the radio show. It shot to number three on Memphis's country and western charts, and hit the number-one position by the end of the year. The record's success provided Elvis with a few more bookings, both alone or with Scotty and Bill's band, the Starlight Wranglers. Elvis, howev-

er, wasn't taking any chances. He still showed up for work every day at Crown Electric.

Less than two weeks after the release of "That's All Right," Elvis performed at the Overton Park Shell, an open-air auditorium in Memphis. He was the opening act for Slim Whitman, an established country performer. Nervous and eager to please, Elvis threw all his energy into "That's All Right." The only thing that mattered was getting the song right and Elvis was concentrating—hard. But he began hearing strange screeches and screams. Although the noise threatened to drown out the music, Elvis forged ahead, unable to decipher its meaning. The screams continued throughout "Blue Moon of Kentucky" and continued even after he'd left the stage. Without knowing it, Elvis and his little band had brought down the house. And the audience at the Overton Shell had seen Elvis's famous stage gyrations for the first time.

In an interview in *TV Guide* two years later, Elvis explained what happened that night. "I came out on stage and I was scared stiff. It was my first big appearance in front of an audience. I was doing a fast-type tune, one of my first records, and everybody was hollerin' and I didn't know what they were hollering at. Everybody was screaming and everything. When I came offstage, my manager told me they were hollerin' because I was wigglin' my legs. I was unaware. I went back out for an encore and I did a little more, and the more I did the louder it went."

Elvis's first hit was "That's All Right" on the Sun Records label. It was Memphis disc jockey Dewey Phillips, shown here with Elvis, who first played the record on the air.

RADIO TAKES OVER

Elvis's success was confined to the Memphis area, but it turned out to be his ticket to radio's most popular country and western music show, the "Grand Ole Opry." A successful audition for the Opry meant instant success for a musical performer. Every kid who picked up a guitar dreamed of making it to the Opry. Usually it took years for a performer to get to that stage in Nashville, but with the immediate success of his first record Elvis made it in just a four-hour drive from Memphis.

Conservative, traditional, family-oriented—those words describe the audience and the performers at the Grand Ole Opry. With his flamboyant clothes and flashy stage manners—Chet Atkins, the great country and western guitarist remembers his shock at Elvis's eye shadow—the Hillbilly Cat must have looked like something from another planet. The bewildered Nashville audience sat through his set and applauded politely. Elvis wasn't even that well received, however, with the Opry's booking agent and manager, Jim Denny. When the show was over, Denny told Elvis that they didn't do that kind of music at the Opry. "If I were you," Denny said, "I'd go back to driving a truck."

Elvis had bombed, badly, for the first time in his career, although it seems obvious that it wasn't really his fault. The Opry was clearly not ready for him. Nevertheless, he broke down and cried bitter tears of disappointment on his way back to Memphis. Elvis always remembered that night. Later in his career he said that Jim Denny broke his heart.

Elvis's second radio show, the less traditional "Louisiana Hayride," proved quite a bit more successful. Elvis and the Blue Moon Boys, as they were now calling themselves, were invited back for the next weekend and even offered a one-year contract. Like the Opry, the Hayride often took beginning singers and made them into regional stars because of the wide popularity of the broadcasts.

*Elvis in performance. Scotty Moore
of the Blue Moon Boys is on guitar.*

Also like the Opry, the Louisiana Hayride paid its performers nothing more than union scale, which meant eighteen
dollars per show for Elvis and twelve dollars each for Bill and
Scotty. The money hardly covered the expenses of getting
back and forth to Shreveport, Louisiana, but the real payoff
came with the recognition and bookings. The Hayride was
broadcast on KWKH over most of the South and South-
west.

Through the show's booking bureau, Elvis began to get
more frequent engagements, working package tours with
better-known performers. Now billed as "The Hillbilly Cat" or
"The King of Western Bop," Elvis felt secure enough to quit
his job at Crown Electric. He continued to record at Sun, and
had more than enough work to keep him busy. There were
endless one-night stands in Louisiana, Texas, and Arkansas.
The trio spent long hours on the road and slept in their cars,
or in cheap motels if they had enough money.

A hard life, but, despite the difficulties, Elvis loved it. He
was bringing a new and novel kind of music—his music—to
people who had barely heard of it before. Each new audience
demanded a good show from the boys and they did their
best to deliver the goods. Yet, with all the screaming crowds
and the popular records, he still wasn't making a living. In
fact, almost all of the money went into gas for the cars and
food and shelter for the band.

Sam Phillips didn't go on the road, so Scotty Moore took
over as Elvis's manager. Scotty was supposed to ward off
unscrupulous show business types who might take advan-
tage of Elvis. After six months, Scotty sold his contract to the
more experienced Bob Neal, a popular and hardworking
Memphis disc jockey. Neal not only hosted two radio shows a
day from WMPS (one of them featured Elvis's old friends, the
Blackwood brothers), but he also ran a record store and a
management agency, and put together what he called "promotions." These were small-scale country music jamborees

usually held at schoolhouses within a couple of hours' drive from Memphis. Neal would host the show, opening with a few jokes and a ukulele tune, and then introduce three or four musical acts. People often came to see the shows based on Bob Neal's popularity alone. He would do three or four shows a week, advertising them in advance on his radio shows. In fact, Elvis and the Blue Moon Boys did more than two hundred of these promotions in one year with Bob Neal. The usual evening's take, to be divided by everyone, would be around three hundred dollars.

The work was grueling but steady, and the money began to get better. Elvis soon bought the first of many Cadillacs, a secondhand model that caught fire on a trip back from Texarkana. Elvis had its successor painted pink and black, a color combination that later became his trademark. With the money flowing in, he quickly fulfilled two lifelong dreams. He bought his first brand-new pink Cadillac and set up his parents in a little brick house on Lamar Avenue in Memphis.

The constant touring forced Elvis to polish his stage show and taught him the importance of not quitting till the crowd was won over. He developed a set of stage tricks that would serve him well throughout his career. Sprinting out to center stage, he would turn on the sultry stare, start pumping those legs and lean back with an extended "Wellllllll." By itself, this opener often turned on the screams before the first song had actually begun. Whether the show was big or small, at an arena in Jacksonville or a schoolhouse in Mississippi, Elvis and the boys never quit until the audience had been whipped into a frenzy.

Though he spent much of his time on the road, Elvis continued to record at Sun studios. His second release was another hopped-up version of a rhythm and blues tune, this time "Good Rocking Tonight," by Wynonie Harris. An equally rhythmic treatment of a country standard, "I Don't Care If the Sun Don't Shine," filled out the "B" side. The single went to number three on the Memphis charts. This musical mix seemed like a formula for success.

The third Sun release, "Milkcow Boogie Blues," was an even older tune. First recorded in 1930, this song was later livened up by Joe Williams, one of the forerunners of rock and roll. On this recording from Elvis's Sun sessions, some dialogue that was recorded reveals Elvis's growing confidence in his own musical intuition.

The song at first just shuffles along, not doing much of anything rhythmically, when Elvis interrupts. "Hold it, fellas. That don't move me. Let's get real, real gone for a change." He then proceeds to whip the song up into a charging tempo, and freely improvises with the melody and lyrics. Now, the song becomes transformed, reborn as an early rock and roll classic. Throughout his entire career, Elvis continued to work this way, relying on his intuition. Often, a song was recorded over and over again while he touched up the details. "I take my time to do the right thing," Elvis explained later. "It begins with listening and more listening. I listen for hours, for a week, two weeks. When I'm down to the songs I think I'll want to do, I call the session." He didn't give up until it felt right, and even much later in his career would often stay at the studio long after everyone else had gone home, begging for one more try.

Even though "Milkcow Boogie Blues" is one of the best efforts to come from the Sun studio days, the record sold poorly. Perhaps the novelty had worn off. To Elvis, this just proved that Bob Neal was right when he said that a singer had to go out and perform live to sell records.

It was Bob Neal who lent Elvis out for his biggest package tour yet, the Hank Snow Jamboree. The shows took him through Louisiana, Alabama, Georgia, Florida, Virginia, and Tennessee. Although he wasn't headlining yet, Elvis's act impressed many people in show business, including Colonel Thomas A. Parker, who managed, booked, and promoted the jamboree. Known throughout the South as simply "the Colonel," Parker knew a rising star when he saw one. He also knew he would soon take charge of Elvis's career.

THE COLONEL

The stories about supersalesman Tom Parker go like this: working the traveling carnivals as a young man, the Colonel sold foot-long hot dogs with nothing but mustard and relish in the middle and two little pieces of wiener sticking out each end. And he got away with it. Such were his powers of persuasion that he unloaded sparrows painted yellow as canaries. As a hasty substitute for an act that didn't show up, he advertised "dancing chickens." They danced alright, but what the locals didn't know was that the Colonel set the birds down on an electric hot plate, while he played a recording of "Turkey in the Straw."

With his portly physique—even as a young man—the Colonel has often been compared to W. C. Fields, with whom he shared some other traits. The most fitting comparison, however, is to another American original, P. T. Barnum. Barnum, of course, was the founder of the Barnum and Bailey Circus, which later joined forces with the Ringling Bros. to become "The Greatest Show on Earth." It was Barnum who said, "There's a sucker born every minute." That could have been the Colonel's motto as well.

Tom Parker's real education began when he started working for the Royal American Shows in his early twenties. The Royal American was the best, the biggest, the grandest carnival in the world. Traveling with its own seventy-car train—hauling over a thousand people, huge rides, generators, tractors, tents, scaffolding—the show would barrel across the country, stopping in dozens of towns and cities for their annual fairs.

Colonel Parker worked with the Royal American for

almost a decade. His traveling companions were snake charmers, midgets, sword swallowers, geeks (who bit off the heads of live chickens), as well as the usual array of freaks and hucksters who would con the customers into pitching baseballs, shooting rifles, doing whatever gave the carnival a good chance of separating a fool from his money.

In the mid-1930s, Colonel Parker retired from the carny and set himself up in Tampa, Florida, where the National spent the winter. At first he sold his services as a press agent and publicist to circuses, riverboat shows, other carnivals, or anybody who needed his carny-bred savvy. Apparently down on his luck, the Colonel later took a job as a dogcatcher a few years later with the Hillsborough County Humane Society. He loved animals, and the job also came with a free apartment above the shelter. His publicity skills served him well in this job, too. More than once, a photograph of him rescuing a poor helpless pet turned up in the local paper. He also raised enough money to rebuild the kennel.

It wasn't much of a jump then to promoting country singers when they visited Tampa. Minnie Pearl, the country and western comedienne, met the Colonel in the 1940s, and hired him as an "advance man" for the tent shows that she took on the road. Colonel Parker would arrive a few days ahead of the show, plastering the town with flyers and handbills and scaring up radio coverage. He would sometimes employ elephants and midgets to create the hurly-burly excitement of the circus coming to town. From the start though, the Colonel had his eye on a promising young singer on the tour, Eddy Arnold, who was known as the Tennessee Plowboy.

The Colonel saw commercial potential in Arnold, and convinced the young singer to hire him as his manager. The terms of the contract were generous to the Colonel, but for a reason: he took on only one client at a time and devoted all his energies to his charge. Their nine-year relationship brought Arnold to the very top of country and western music charts. When they parted in 1953, the Colonel retired to his home in Madison, Tennessee—temporarily. Before very long, he was working with the country singer who had the number one song of 1954. He took over Hank Snow Enterprises, an organization built around the popular little singer from Nova Scotia, Canada.

In April of 1955, Elvis's fourth single on Sun, "Baby, Let's Play House," made it to the national charts. By July it had climbed to number ten on *Billboard*'s country chart, just as his fifth and last single on Sun Records, "Mystery Train," was released. Throughout the year, the Colonel watched and listened to this new phenomenon. Somewhere along the way he decided that Elvis would be his next star. Even after he decided, though, he waited cautiously to make his move. His scouts had told him a little bit about this boy. Despite his wild stage image, he was a loyal and obedient son who relied on his parents' judgment. The Colonel knew that Gladys and Vernon would have to be won over first.

A meeting was arranged with Elvis, his father, and Bob Neal, who was still officially Elvis's manager. The Colonel offered his advice on their plans for the fall and winter. They decided that Elvis had outgrown his days at tiny Sun Records; he would have to sign with a larger record company that could promote him nationally.

The Colonel boasted of his credentials and connections, and he quickly won over Vernon Presley by telling him his boy was working too hard and for too little money. Gladys, suspicious by nature and protective of Elvis, proved a little harder to get to, but the Colonel bided his time. Bob Neal agreed to turn over the management chores to the Colonel, in exchange for a percentage of Elvis's new record contract, which the Colonel figured would draw some fifty thousand dollars.

Fifty thousand dollars! That was more money than the Presleys had hoped to see in a lifetime. Throughout the year,

Elvis's manager, Colonel Tom Parker, was a master
salesman. When interviewed by the press in January
of 1957, he said of Elvis, "He's like most other
twenty-one-year-old fellows. He has a few dates, takes
care of his folks, and tries hard to live right."

as Elvis's popularity grew, the major record companies had expressed some interest in buying out Sam Phillips's recording contract. But Sam's original offer to sell for $4,000 was literally laughed off. Later, when it became obvious that Elvis was not a flash in the pan, Sam asked as much as $20,000. A bandleader named Mitch Miller, who was very influential in popular music at the time, heard Sam's $20,000 offer and slammed down the phone in a huff.

Now it was Colonel Parker's turn to peddle Elvis to the big boys up North. Armed with an agreement from Elvis's parents giving him the right to negotiate a record deal, he flew to New York. Almost immediately, RCA Records, who had profited from Eddy Arnold's success, succumbed to the Colonel's powers of persuasion. They offered $35,000 plus a $5,000 personal bonus to Elvis for signing with the company. Sam Phillips flew up from Memphis and agreed to the deal.

Now Gladys became convinced that the Colonel was the right man to manage her boy. He became a personal adviser and agent to Elvis. Bob Neal was still officially Elvis's manager, but that wouldn't last much longer. The Colonel was running the show now.

FAME

4

By September, 1955, Elvis had three songs on the national charts. Teenagers all over the country were buying his records. When his contract was officially signed in November, RCA re-released all five of the Sun singles to a national audience. The money began pouring in!

Elvis's first reaction? He bought another new home for his parents, an even bigger house in a nicer part of Memphis. Then he bought for his mother his own symbol of success, a brand-new pink Cadillac. It didn't matter that Gladys didn't drive.

The first RCA recording session took place after the Christmas holidays in January of 1956. This session produced "Heartbreak Hotel," the single which would become Elvis's biggest hit so far. But when the session was over, it was business as usual. Elvis went back on the road with Scotty and Bill, playing one-night stands. While they were traveling, Elvis learned that the Colonel had booked him for six TV appearances on Tommy and Jimmy Dorsey's "Stage Show," a Saturday evening variety program hosted by the big-band brothers.

His first time on the show, Elvis tried mightily to put across on television the excitement that he had stirred up all across the South. He started off with "Blue Suede Shoes," a current hit for Sam Phillips's new rockabilly prodigy, Carl Perkins. Then Elvis went on to sing "Heartbreak Hotel," which was just being released as a single. He used every trick that he knew, summoning up all the moves he had perfected during his years on the road. As usual he gave his all, but this time he was rewarded with indifference: no wild cheering, no screaming girls. The New York studio audience apparently had no idea who this kid was or what he was up to.

The rest of the country's reaction came the next day, in a barrage of letters and telegrams and a flood of phone calls to the CBS-TV switchboard. The people of America were appalled at the spectacle they had witnessed the night before—a greasy haired, oversexed, vulgar hillbilly making primitive music and obscene gestures.

The reaction from the record-buying public was quite the opposite. Within weeks, "Heartbreak Hotel" reached the number-one spot on *Billboard* magazine's pop and country charts and went to number five on the rhythm and blues charts. Controversy was good for ratings as well as record sales, and Elvis sang on "Stage Show" five more times in the winter and spring of 1956. In between appearances on the show, he continued to tour the country, playing to screaming audiences and ever larger hordes of delirious girls.

Elvis was booked on "Stage Show" to bolster the program's sagging ratings. The producers would have tried anything, even shoving rock and roll music into a big-band variety show, but it wasn't the music that appealed to the show's executives. The idea was to capitalize on Elvis's animal magnetism. In explaining his decision to go with an unknown southern singer, one of the producers put it succintly: "This kid is a guitar-playing Marlon Brando."

In September of 1955, Elvis signed a contract with RCA. It was the beginning of a long, profitable association.

The comparison to one of the hottest young movie stars of the day was not lost on the people who make movies out in Hollywood. Just weeks after his final appearance on "Stage Show," movie producer Hal Wallis flew Elvis to California for a screen test.

NEXT STOP HOLLYWOOD

To Elvis, being a rock and roll star paled next to his dreams of being a movie star. Although he had made a name for himself as a guitar-strumming singer, he saw himself primarily as an "entertainer" rather than a musician. James Dean, Tony Curtis, even Rudolph Valentino, the silent film star of the 1920s, were his heroes. Other rock and rollers, Bill Haley, Little Richard, and Carl Perkins, were merely competitors for a teenage audience that was sure to vanish.

In 1956, the current craze for rock music was thought to be a passing fad, and Elvis planned to be around for a long time. Spike Jones, the leader of a popular orchestra that played novelty tunes, put it this way: "I want to count Elvis's hound dogs twenty years from now. Only time will tell if Elvis is collecting Cadillacs in 1976." For all his natural musical talent, Elvis had little confidence that rock music would sustain him and his family in the future. But movie stars could grow old and still work. Finding this type of security was an ideal that his parents had taught him well.

In April of 1956, Elvis and Colonel Parker flew out to Hollywood for the screen test. Director Hal Wallis obviously liked what he saw. He signed Elvis to a three-picture deal with Paramount that started at $100,000 a picture. Wallis, who had produced Humphrey Bogart's *Casablanca* and had discovered the comedy team of Jerry Lewis and Dean Martin, went to work on finding a suitable project for Elvis. In the meantime, he agreed to lend him to Twentieth Century Fox for a film that was gearing up for production. The film was titled *The Reno Brothers,* but it would eventually be named *Love Me Tender.*

While in California, Elvis appeared on NBC's "Milton Berle Show," one of the most popular shows of the 1950s. About forty million people watched Elvis sing "Heartbreak Hotel" and "Blue Suede Shoes." With the beaming approval of America's favorite comedian, Uncle Miltie, Elvis was again presented to a major part of the American population. His popularity skyrocketed, and the record sales soared.

He went right back on the road, however, taking only a few days out to record at RCA's Nashville studios. This session was a fruitful one; the emotional ballad, "I Want You, I Need You, I Love You" quickly became his next number-one hit.

At the end of the month, *Life* magazine devoted a spread to the new star, now billed by the Colonel as "The Nation's First Atomic-Powered Singer." Based on the success of "Heartbreak Hotel," *Life* headlined the picture spread, "Young Elvis Presley's Complaint Becomes Nation's Top Pop Tune." Riding high, Elvis was booked into Las Vegas as an opening act for comedian Shecky Greene and the Freddie Martin Orchestra.

In the mid-1950s, Las Vegas represented to many Americans glamour and sophistication. The vacation spot of the rich and famous, Las Vegas epitomized the post–World War II nightclub style of Frank Sinatra and Dean Martin. When Elvis roared into town, accompanied by all of the carnival atmosphere the Colonel could muster, the middle-aged crowd, if they had any interest at all in this strange phenomenon, came to see him as a curiosity. Members of the audience at the Frontier Hotel were probably wondering what their sons and daughters were raving about.

The Hillbilly Cat did what he always did, but he just couldn't get this audience to react. There was so little response from the crowd that Bill Black said it was the first time they could hear the mistakes in their playing. It was also the first time in Elvis's soaring career (except for his early appearance at the Grand Ole Opry) that he bombed badly, and the six-week contract was torn up after a week. This just wasn't his crowd. Despite the later nationwide adoration that would be his, Elvis never forgot the humiliation of this date. He remained bitter about his Las Vegas reception for years.

Although *Time* and *Newsweek* first noticed him about this time—and gave him mixed but kind reviews—he now became the target for critics who not only considered him a vulgar hillbilly from the South, but a juvenile delinquent and a genuine menace to American youth.

"UNTALENTED AND VULGAR"

Elvis's second appearance on Milton Berle's show gave his critics an even bigger opportunity to mock the new singer. On the show, he sang his new record, "Hound Dog," a song that he had first heard during his disastrous stay in Las Vegas. As always, he put his heart and his soul—and his hips—into it. So did Jack Gould of *The New York Times* in his devastating review. "Mr. Presley has no discernible singing ability," the critic wrote. "His specialty is rhythm songs which he renders in an undistinguished whine. . . . to the ear he is an unutterable bore."

John Crosby of the *New York Herald Tribune* called Elvis "unspeakably untalented and vulgar." At New York's *Journal-American*, critic Jack O'Brien wrote: "He can't sing a lick, makes up for vocal shortcomings with the weirdest, and plainly planned, suggestive animation short of an aborigine's mating dance."

These tastemakers, who undoubtedly thought of themselves as refined people, obviously did not understand Elvis's appeal, but neither did they understand the change taking place in American popular music. This new sound—rock and roll—a threatening confusion of black and white musical styles, became the scapegoat for the perceived problem of "juvenile delinquency." The authorities—teachers, government officials, concerned parents—demonstrated a state of mind that can only be called paranoid. The music was branded atheistic, criminal, and even a threat to democracy.

Typical newspaper headlines from the mid 1950s seriously posed the question:

DOES ROCK AND ROLL CAUSE DELINQUENCY?

Other headlines sounded the alarm this way:

MUSIC OR MADNESS? ROCK AND ROLL MUSIC
HAS STIRRED UP A WHIRLWIND OF ADULT PROTEST

TEENAGE MUSIC CRAZE HAS PARENTS WORRIED—
WE'RE LOSING CONTROL OF OUR CHILDREN

What was happening? Part of the problem stemmed from the accepted racial bigotry of America in the 1950s that was threatened by music that had white teenagers dancing to "race records." In Alabama, the executive director of an organization that called itself the White Citizens Council proudly posed for newsreel cameras to deliver this message:

"The obscenity and vulgarity of the rock and roll music is obviously a means by which the white man and his children are to be driven to the level of the Nigra. And if you choose to call that the Communist idealogy, I think you've hit it fairly on the head."

Rock and roll concerts were banned in San Antonio, Texas; San Jose, California; Jersey City, New Jersey; and in hundreds of small towns and cities. From the principal's office, the pulpit, the editorial pages, and city halls across the country, rock and roll was denounced as an evil and satanic force, and even a Communist conspiracy.

(This 1950s campaign against rock and roll was the first time the music came under attack, but it would hardly be the last. In the late 1960s and early 1970s, the vice president of the United States, Spiro Agnew, enlisted the help of the Federal Bureau of Investigation (FBI) to try to decipher the lyrics of songs that he felt contained hidden messages. Songs that were thought to have references to drug use were banned from the airwaves. In 1985, a small group of women who were married to congressmen and legislators convinced the U.S. Senate to listen closely to rock lyrics. This group wanted songs to be rated like movies, if the lyrics contained any references to sex, drugs, violence, or the occult. They won a victory of sorts when the major record companies agreed to affix warning stickers to albums that were considered unsuitable for children's ears.)

As the most popular rock and roller, Elvis became the target of scorn and organized protest. Images of the young singer were hung in effigy or burned, his records smashed. Several organizations set out to ban him and his music from TV and radio. One group stated pointedly that it wanted to "eliminate" him altogether.

With his long hair, uninhibited sensuality and his devastating effect on young women, Elvis represented perhaps the worst fears of those who sought to "control" their children. But Elvis the rebel was also Elvis the gentleman. He responded to these assaults politely. Critics "had a job to do," he said, just like his job as an entertainer. Even his accusers were addressed as "sir" or "ma'am." One of the few times he reacted angrily to criticism of his music, he responded by saying, "Them critics don't like to see nobody doing any kind of music they don't know nuthin' about. The colored folk been singin' it and playin' it just the way I'm doin' now, man, for more years than I know. Nobody paid it no mind till I goosed it up."

On television, one reporter asked Elvis if he had shot his mother with a gun. For a law-abiding son who loved his mother dearly, this question was beyond his comprehension. Chuckling softly, turning his eyes down from the camera, he replied, "Well, that one takes the cake."

Steve Allen, a smooth-talking and sophisticated television personality of the 1950s, had just begun hosting a variety show to compete with Ed Sullivan's. Allen disliked rock and roll music—and openly made fun of it—but he was not blind to its audience appeal.

Allen booked Elvis for his show, and decided to make a fool of the young singer. Elvis was pressured to appear in corny "hillbilly" skits designed to mock his Southern heritage. In another segment, he was dressed in a tuxedo with tails, to sing "Hound Dog" to a basset hound that sat on a stool. Even *Newsweek*, no fan of Elvis's, found the TV host's motives "questionable." The singer, however, took it like a good sport. He "did his job," and left the show still riding the wave of his ever increasing popularity.

The successful TV host Ed Sullivan once vowed he would never have Elvis on his show. But after Elvis's appearance on his rival's show got most of the country watching, Sullivan changed his mind. The Colonel squeezed the then outrageous sum of $50,000 from Sullivan for three performances. On September 9, 1956 Elvis played for fifty-four million Americans, roughly 80 percent of the entire viewing audience.

On this show, Elvis introduced "Love Me Tender," the title song from his first motion picture, scheduled to open in two months. Even though RCA had released seven 45-rpm singles of songs that had been on Elvis's first album, the public clamored for more. They could not get enough. Close to a million orders came in for "Love Me Tender." Elvis now boasted three number-one singles in a row. By the end of

1956, he would have seventeen records on the charts. Nothing like this had ever been seen in popular music, this much popularity so fast.

Later that month, on September 27, 1956, a triumphant twenty-two-year-old Elvis Presley came home to Tupelo, Mississippi. The occasion was "Elvis Presley Day," part of the Mississippi-Alabama Fair and Dairy Show. The hero's welcome he received was particularly sweet because in 1945, at the age of ten, he first sang in public at this fair. He still remembered the five-dollar prize and free admission to every ride in the amusement park. After a parade through the main streets, Elvis received a guitar-shaped key to the city. In return, he signed over his $10,000 check to the town of Tupelo.

ELVIS THE STAR

Elvis's first movie, *Love Me Tender*, opened in New York on November 15 with what was now the usual amount of fanfare. A thirty-foot cardboard cutout of the teen idol was unveiled for the throngs of teenagers who had gathered on the streets for the movie's first showing. Twentieth Century Fox anticipated so much box office business that it made and shipped more prints of this film than it had ever done for any other movie.

Elvis appeared on Steve Allen's TV variety show on June 29, 1956. Dressed in tuxedo with tails at Allen's request, he sang "Hound Dog" to a passive basset hound sitting on a stool.

In 1956, twenty-two-year-old Elvis returned to Tupelo, Mississippi, his birthplace, to perform before thousands at the Mississippi-Alabama Fair and Dairy Show.

Elvis sang four songs in the movie, a quickly made Civil War story that recovered its cost of $1 million in its first three days. The critics, once again, had a field day. *Time* magazine wrote: "Is it a sausage? It is certainly smooth and damp looking but who ever heard of a 172-pound sausage six-feet tall?" The review went on to savage Elvis's performance, at one point asking about his singing, "A voice? Or merely a noise produced, like the voice of a cricket, by the violent stridulations of the legs?"

Despite the protestations from critics and other adults, Elvis's popularity grew even wider. His farewell concert for the "Louisiana Hayride," the radio show that had helped launch him as an unknown just a year before, nearly caused a full-scale riot as nine thousand teenagers kept up a steady roar throughout his performance. Elvis's image and name were everywhere now, thanks to the merchandising skills of the Colonel. Everything from Hound Dog–Orange lipstick to Elvis jeans, shirts, socks, and record cases could be purchased by avid fans. All of this, of course, was in addition to the usual array of posters and statuettes. Elvis closed out the year in a blur, as he continued the fastest rise to stardom that show business had ever seen.

The famous third appearance on the "Ed Sullivan Show" took place in the first week after the New Year holiday. For this show Elvis was photographed from the waist up in an attempt to appease the CBS censors. It didn't work, though. With seven Elvis songs featured that Sunday night, it was more like the "Elvis Presley Show" than the "Ed Sullivan Show."

The blinding pace continued. Only weeks later, Elvis returned to Hollywood to begin filming his second movie, *Loving You.* Elvis was pleased to have his parents with him this time, and they stayed for a month. Gladys got herself dolled up, and even bought a poodle—just like the fancy Hol-

*Elvis's hometown, Memphis, Tennessee, was the
site of the world premiere of the movie*
Loving You *on July 9, 1957. A packed house of
happy Elvis fans screamed with delight.* Facing
page: *Hollywood actress Natalie Wood arrives
in Memphis to visit Elvis in October of 1956.*

lywood movie stars that she had read about in magazines. This was one of the happiest times in his mother's life. The little family was together, and thanks to her darling little boy, they had made it from the slums of East Tupelo to Hollywood Boulevard.

Once he became acquainted with Hollywood, Elvis began to date the most popular young actresses, starting with Debra Paget, who would costar in a few movies with him, and later Natalie Wood. These beautiful young stars belonged to a crowd that was known to be wild. They were the Hollywood version of beatniks, the "brat pack" of their day. James Dean, the star of *Rebel Without a Cause,* was their hero. They were sophisticated and "cool" in a way that attracted a country boy like Elvis, just like he had been attracted to the flashy clothes at Lansky's. And what was remarkable to Elvis, even though he was by far the hottest young performer in the country, they accepted him. Nick Adams, who was once a friend of actor James Dean, became especially close.

Both Natalie Wood and Nick Adams accepted invitations to come to Memphis, where Elvis entertained them as he would his other friends. For some time, Elvis had been renting movie theaters, skating rinks, and amusement parks after closing time so that he and his entourage could enjoy themselves without hordes of fans. The Hollywood set who came along for these activities were amazed that the clean-cut image that Elvis portrayed for the press was actually true. He didn't smoke or drink and politely signed autographs for hours every night.

The whole Presley family now lived in Graceland, a twenty-three-room mansion on thirteen acres at the top of a hill in the affluent Memphis suburb of Whitehaven. Elvis bought the house for $100,000 in March of 1957, not simply because it was bigger, but because it afforded the family some privacy. Graceland was a bit run-down when the Presleys bought it,

Elvis stands by his new Rolls Royce in front of Graceland,
his twenty-three-room mansion in a Memphis suburb.

but within a few months it would be transformed into a poor Southern boy's vision of elegance. Huge columns framed the Georgian entrance, and inside it was decorated with plush fabrics and carpets in the style of the newly wealthy. But out back, Gladys and Vernon planted a little garden to grow their own vegetables, and added a chicken coop.

In July 1957, as *Loving You* premiered, Elvis had just finished filming *Jailhouse Rock*, his third movie. In this film, Elvis portrays an ex-convict who becomes a singing sensation but signs away half of all his earnings to a savvy older man while still in prison. This movie, like the ones before it, stuck to a formula. Elvis plays a character, much like one side of himself, who bursts into song at the unlikeliest times. Although Elvis did have some natural acting ability, his movies required little more than his name and a few songs.

The song-and-dance number built around the title tune, "Jailhouse Rock," represents one of the high points of Elvis's early movie career. His natural stage mannerisms are choreographed into an elegant stylized modern-dance number that shows off Elvis's natural ability. Dancing, singing, and flinging himself around the two-story stage setting with grace and control, Elvis could easily have been mistaken for a professional dancer. He was only twenty-two.

By October, not only was the *Loving You* sound track the top-selling album in the country, but "(Let Me Be Your) Teddy Bear" hung in the top-ten singles chart. "Jailhouse Rock," just released, was on its way to becoming the number-one

In the song-and-dance sequence for the movie Jailhouse Rock, *Elvis demonstrated a grace and style not evident until then.*

song in the country, right as the movie opened. If all this wasn't enough, Elvis capped another successful tour with a pair of sold-out concerts in Hollywood's Pan-Pacific Auditorium.

At the Hollywood concerts, he set out to show the movie executives and his new actor friends what he could do with a *live* audience. The first show was so wild that the police were called. They trained cameras on his hips, determined to arrest him for the slightest "obscene" gesture. At the start of his second show he pointed out the movie cameras to the audience and made a halo around his head with his hands. "I'm gonna be an angel tonight," he said. The crowd roared before the first note sounded. In just twelve months, twenty-two-year-old Elvis Presley had turned the entertainment business on its ear.

DRAFTED

Throughout 1957, there had been rumors that Elvis would be drafted into the armed services. He had taken his physical examination amid much publicity, and was declared fit for service. On December 20, Elvis received his draft notice. Counseled by the Colonel to do so, Elvis agreed to serve in the army, not in the special services as an entertainer, but as a soldier. That meant no concerts, no performing. Even though Elvis's career was soaring, the Colonel, it seems, thought it wise to send Elvis away for two years to prove a point: that he was really a good boy and a good American.

Elvis, shorn of his sideburns and wavy hair, arrives at Fort Chaffee, Arkansas, to begin his hitch in the Army.

Elvis with his parents, Vernon and Gladys
Presley. On the eve of his induction into
the Army in 1958, Elvis gives his mother
a farewell kiss. She died later that year.

Elvis did as he was told.

On March 24, 1958, the fastest-rising career in show business history slammed to a halt. Elvis was inducted into the army and shipped to Fort Chaffee, Arkansas, and then to Fort Hood, Texas, for indoctrination. Every step of the way, from the haircut to his physical examination, was documented by photographers, with the Colonel standing by, watching.

Elvis knew from the start that he would serve much of his hitch overseas. On June 10, during a leave, he went into the recording studio for the last time until 1960. During his time in the army, RCA would rerelease much of his earlier material, along with some of the songs from this session, including "A Big Hunk of Love." His fans remained loyal to the soldier boy; the records sold millions.

Gladys Presley, who had never learned to bear any extended separation from her son, became sick with grief at the thought of Elvis's departure. Even though Elvis had arranged for his family and friends to stay in a rented house near Fort Hood, Gladys's condition worsened. She knew he was going to be away from her for months. She feared that something terrible was going to happen to Elvis. On the evening before Elvis was scheduled to embark for Germany, Gladys broke down physically. Elvis sent her and Vernon back to Memphis to be taken care of by her own doctor. Her skin had turned yellow from a liver ailment that the doctors could not diagnose. She was immediately put into the hospital.

Gladys's health problems were not at all helped by her unhealthy diet. All her life she was overweight, and although she told few people, she took amphetamines as diet pills and also drank. But whatever the physical reasons for her "grieving," it was Elvis's imminent departure that turned her for the worse.

When he realized how seriously ill his mother had become, Elvis tried frantically to get a leave. Denied permission again and again, he made up his mind to go home anyway. His leave came through soon after, though, and he stayed by his mother's bedside for three days. When she appeared to be recovering, he went out to the movies. At 3:00 A.M. Vernon called from the hospital to tell his son that Gladys had died of a heart attack.

Elvis had lost his inspiration and his foundation. Gladys had been the most important figure in his life, the parent who had never left him. Their bond was so strong that he grieved over her loss for years, just as she had done for his twin brother, Jesse Garon. He had to be physically pulled away from her coffin on the day she was buried. Gladys's death was a loss that profoundly affected Elvis the rest of his life.

Nevertheless, Elvis was in the army now, and he went off to Germany like a good soldier. Landing in the northern port city of Bremen, Private Presley traveled by troop train to the U.S. Army base in Friedberg, about an hour north of Frankfurt. Cheering fans met him along the way, assuring *Der Elvis* that he was still the King of rock and roll, even if temporarily in exile.

Elvis was lonely in Germany, and as soon as he could, he sent for his family and friends. They settled in the nearby town of Bad Neuheim, and set up a home as well as an office to take care of Elvis's business affairs and answer fan mail. He spent most of his time off at the little house, holding sing-alongs just as he had done in Graceland. He signed autographs every evening in front of his new home, determined to remain true to his fans whether they were in Germany or America.

PRISCILLA

Despite these attempts to make Germany his home, Elvis remained lonely. He never ate his meals away from home or the base and hardly ever went out. He was not very happy.

That is, until he met fourteen-year-old Priscilla Beaulieu, the beautiful and precocious stepdaughter of U.S. Air Force captain Paul Beaulieu and his wife, Ann, who were stationed about an hour's drive from Elvis's German home-away-from-home.

"She looks like an angel," Elvis exclaimed when he saw her. With her relatively heavy makeup, womanly figure, and dark brown hair, Priscilla did look more mature than her years, but even when he found out how old she was, it mattered little to all concerned. In the South, it wasn't uncommon for girls in their midteens to be considered eligible. Elvis introduced himself awkwardly and asked Priscilla if she went to school.

"Ninth," Priscilla answered.

Confused by her answer, Elvis asked, "Ninth what?"

"Grade," Priscilla responded.

When Elvis remarked for others to hear that she was just a baby, the sensitive teenager huffed sarcastically, "Thanks."

Elvis was charmed by the spunky Priscilla. He sat down at the piano and began to sing directly to her. The fourteen-year-old girl noticed that if she looked away, he tried all the harder to impress her. She went home that night to tell her parents what had happened—that the famous Elvis Presley had paid attention to her—although she could hardly believe it herself. Needless to say, Captain and Mrs. Beaulieu did not approve.

Even so, it wasn't long after this meeting that Priscilla began spending two and three evenings a week with Elvis and his family, arriving home well into the night with the car and driver Elvis had provided for her. Her parents had become even more upset and asked to meet Elvis.

When he wanted something, Elvis could be very persuasive. He had become obsessed with 'Cilla, as he called her, and wanted to spend even more time with her. After meeting him, Priscilla's mother and stepfather were convinced that Elvis was telling the truth when he said that he would "do right" by her. Elvis brought his father to further assure Captain and Mrs. Beaulieu that all the activities at Elvis's German home were innocent. And indeed, except for some kissing and cuddling in his upstairs bedroom, they were just that.

Priscilla, for her part, was not the typical fourteen-year-old. She was determined from the first to hold on to her new love, despite the insurmountable obstacles she faced: Elvis had a girlfriend back home, he was ten years older than she, and he would be going back to the States within six months to resume his career as the sexiest singer and movie star on earth. In fact, 'Cilla demonstrated from the very beginning the strength of will that drew Elvis to her.

For Elvis, Priscilla was perfect. Although he might be considered the sexiest man on earth, he found himself most comfortable with adoring teenaged girls. He deemed himself trustworthy with their affections and indeed at this time in his life, he was. A young beauty like Priscilla represented a chance for Elvis to relive his own teenage years—when he was as shy and awkward as any boy that age—in comfort and confidence. Beyond that she *was* special. Elvis saw something in her that would stand the test of time.

While in the army, Elvis began another relationship, a destructive one—with drugs. He took Dexedrine, "pep pills," to stay awake during guard duty and maneuvers. At the time, the harmful effects of amphetamines were not widely publicized and this practice seemed acceptable; the other soldiers did it, and some sergeants actually gave them out to their men.

As an entertainer on the road for two years, he had probably taken pep pills before. To a young man, they must have seemed harmless. He even offered a handful to Priscilla to keep up her energy when their long evenings began to affect her schoolwork. Priscilla recalls that Elvis, who had always been plagued by insomnia, also began taking sleeping pills once he was drafted.

ON THE ROAD AGAIN

In March 1960, Elvis was honorably discharged from the army. He flew into Fort Dix, New Jersey, where he was met by a mob of his fans, a celebration, and Colonel Parker. The Colonel had arranged for a private railroad car to take Elvis home to Memphis. (Elvis hated to fly, and avoided it as long as he could even when touring.) Thousands of fans greeted the returning hero at every whistle-stop in every little town. Trim, fit, and handsome in his dress blues, Sergeant Presley stood on the platform of the railroad car, smiling and waving. At every station, as the train pulled out, the Colonel scattered eight-by-ten glossies in their wake.

While he was away, Elvis always worried that his fans would forget him. He confided this to only a few people, including Priscilla. The reception when the train pulled into Memphis must have brought a smile of reassurance to his face. Thousands of teenagers tried to mob him, and the police had to escort his caravan to Graceland. RCA had received over a million orders for his next record—before it was even recorded—and Frank Sinatra had offered him $125,000 for a six-minute guest appearance on his next television special—to sing two songs! He was still the King.

Elvis had been out of the country during a terrible time for rock and roll. First came the "payola" scandal, in which record companies were caught paying money to disc jockeys to play their records. One of the major figures to fall during the "payola" scandal was Alan Freed, the most important DJ in the history of rock and roll. (In fact "rock and roll" was a term that he coined for the new music, although it existed before as a black euphemism for sex.) Freed had brought black rhythm-and-blues and then rock and roll to white teenagers with his radio show, "The Big Beat," first in Cleveland and later in New York. He was the first DJ to play "Heartbreak Hotel" in New York. Freed was convicted of conspiracy charges for accepting money to play records; his career was ruined.

The first generation of rockers had also fallen on hard times during Elvis's tour of duty. On February 3, 1959, Buddy Holly, the immensely talented Texas-born singer and songwriter of "Peggy Sue," perished in a plane crash while on tour. Richie Valens ("La Bamba"), and the Big Bopper ("Chantilly Lace") also died in the crash. Jerry Lee Lewis, who had scored a major hit for Sam Phillips's Sun records with "Whole Lotta Shakin' Goin' On," ruined his career when he freely admitted to British reporters that he had married his thirteen-year-old cousin, Myra Brown.

The original wild man of rock, Little Richard, left music for the ministry, with the Internal Revenue Service in hot pursuit for back taxes. Chuck Berry, whose songs were recorded by the Beatles and the Rolling Stones, was arrested for transporting a young girl across state lines for "immoral purposes." He served two years in prison. Eddie Cochran perished in a London car accident that crippled Gene Vincent, the singer of "Be Bop a Lula."

A new generation of teen idols had come along to fill the void, but for the most part, they were fresh-faced imposters, groomed by their managers to sing bland, bankable music. The new heartthrobs—Frankie Avalon, Fabian, and others— were not only drawing crowds and selling records—they elicited the same screams from females that Elvis did. It was as if the establishment had prevailed, defusing the "threat of rock and roll" by substituting wax figures—and American teenagers didn't even know the difference.

"The first thing I have to do is press some records," Elvis told reporters as he arrived back in the States. And he did. But his first wave of big hits after coming out of the service had little to do with rock and roll. The payola scandal had apparently convinced the Colonel to steer Elvis toward a more lasting image and career as a crooner.

"It's Now or Never," a tune based on the operatic "O Solo Mio," sold nine million copies, but it was hardly rock and roll. "Are You Lonesome Tonight?," another sugary ballad, sold five million copies. Gone was the urgency of the early hits, the thrill of pushing back the barriers of acceptability. In its place, though, a more skillful, confident voice told listeners that Elvis wasn't kidding when he cited the great opera singer Mario Lanza as one of his main influences.

His first postservice TV appearance on Frank Sinatra's special saw Elvis once again dressed in a tuxedo, and once again looking nervous and ill at ease. The pairing of Elvis with Sinatra, the bobby-soxers' idol of the 1940s was brilliant marketing. The two stars did duets, and Elvis even sang one of Frank's hits, "Witchcraft." The show garnered the ratings the sponsors had expected, but Elvis once again did not escape a critical drubbing from *The New York Times*: "There was nothing morally reprehensible about his performance, it was merely awful."

But the Colonel hatched a new plan by this time. Elvis would broaden and secure his popularity by taking off the rough edges and concentrate on making "pickchas." Elvis went off to make his first post-army movie, *G.I. Blues*, in 1961, and he did not perform in public again for eight years. Instead, he appeared in twenty-one low budget films (which almost always had sound track albums). These moneymakers would turn up in movie theaters during the Christmas and Easter holidays, and, of course, during summer.

Aside from the rare exception of *Viva Las Vegas!*, these

movies are dull-witted low-budget quickies. Some of them took less than three weeks to make. All followed a strict, guaranteed-to-make-money formula: Elvis, playing the outsider or the underdog, pursues a love interest (the latest starlet) at some exotic location, and bursts into song eight or nine times during the film, whether the plot calls for it or not. His costume defines the character. He appears in these movies as: a rodeo rider and carnival hand, a hillbilly, an air force officer, trapeze artist, race car driver, airline pilot, navy frogman, and a boxer.

The scripts were written in Hollywood especially for Elvis, with places blocked out for songs, sometimes even with suggested titles. These titles were then sent to songwriters who would write the tunes, record them on "demo" records and pass them along to RCA. In fact, the whole process was more like an assembly line than a creative endeavor.

The Colonel, who didn't even bother to see many of these movies, once returned a script to a director who made the mistake of asking for his guidance. Impatient with this kind of "artistic" nonsense, he told the director to just go ahead and make his movie; "All we want is songs for an album." The strategy proved to be profitable. Elvis, and his manager, made millions during these years, both from his movie contracts and the sound track albums.

But by 1963 all was not well with the former King of rock and roll. Elvis had tired of the routine of cranking out three mediocre movies a year—with horrible songs—but he never held out for better scripts until much later in his career. He

In 1964, Elvis starred opposite Ann-Margret in Viva Las Vegas!, *one of his most successful films.*

was making $5 million to $6 million a year, largely from the films, and said at the time, "I'd be a fool to tamper with that kind of success." By 1963, Elvis Presley was the highest paid entertainer in show business.

Why he continued to make these silly movies when he was unhappy and bored is a question without a simple answer. The Colonel, who maintained absolute control over Elvis's business affairs, set up the movie deals. But also, Elvis feared that all of his wealth and fame could disappear at any time, a childhood worry that his father continually reinforced. Vernon Presley, even living off his son's wealth, continually harped on the fact that Elvis spent too much money. Vernon would complain and moan, and even pinch pennies with the employees who worked for the Presley family.

Elvis usually responded to his father's carping by spending even more, but to Priscilla and others who were close to him, he confessed his own fear that one day he would be back driving a truck. Perhaps the most important reason Elvis stayed in Hollywood was that he felt himself to be out of step, musically, with the times. In the early 1960s, a revitalized rock and roll had emerged from England, with the Beatles in the forefront. Elvis may have started his career as a rebel, but by now he represented the establishment.

Elvis had kept an eye on the Beatles since the English invasion began. By this time, he had virtually abandoned rock and roll, but his records continued to sell. He watched the record charts constantly, tracking the progress of these new barbarians who copied his early style.

What Elvis didn't know was that the Beatles genuinely idolized him. On tour in 1965, they sought him out in Los Angeles. Awed into silence by meeting their hero, the four Englishmen fumbled their introductions and gushed their admiration. Elvis, just as uncomfortable with the new challengers, only loosened up when they broke out some instruments and jammed on the Beatles hit "I Feel Fine." John Lennon later said, "The only person that we wanted to meet in the United States of America was Elvis Presley."

A few years later, Lennon took the measure of Elvis's place in the history of rock music with this simple but elegant tribute:

"Before Elvis, there was nothing."

THE
KING

5

During the mid-1960s Elvis lived in California, to be near the movie studios. As usual, he kept a large entourage of family and friends around him. This group of seven to twelve young men, most of them old friends from Memphis, Elvis called "the guys." In Hollywood, they came to be known as the "Memphis Mafia," even though two of them weren't from Memphis but were Elvis's former army buddies.

Charlie Hodge, a 5-foot 3-inch (1.6 m) guitarist and singer, took charge of Elvis's musical affairs, and remained a trusted and close friend from the time they met in Germany. Joe Esposito, another army buddy, became Elvis's road manager, bodyguard, and closest aide. Red West, Elvis's high-school friend and protector, later wrote several songs for Elvis, and he remained a bodyguard. Red's cousin, Sonny West, a good-looking Memphis man, helped out with travel arrangements and doubled as a bodyguard and stuntman in several of Elvis's films.

The entourage also included Elvis's cousins, Gene and Billy Smith, who were assigned by Gladys years before to watch over Elvis, particularly during his chronic sleepwalking episodes. Lamar Fike, a 270-pound (122.5 kg) giant who had lived in Germany with the Presley household, had long been on the payroll for no particular reason, but later ran the lights for Elvis's Las Vegas shows. There were assorted others who did little or nothing for Elvis except furnish companionship when he required it.

He required it all the time. The "King's men" provided a security blanket for Elvis in alien surroundings such as Los Angeles. Back home at Graceland, they did whatever Elvis did—watched movies all night at one of the theaters Elvis rented after hours, or played rough games at the Roller-drome. If Elvis was in the mood, they'd play touch football or fight "wars" with fireworks. Elvis liked to have his boyish fun in groups, and he paid each of these men a salary—and often lavished cars and other gifts upon them—to accompany him during his shenanigans.

PRISCILLA

Priscilla had moved into Graceland in 1962, at the age of fifteen, with her parents' permission and approval. She lived in a part of the house with Elvis's Aunt Delta and his grandmother, whom he had nicknamed Dodger because she moved so fast. During those years, Priscilla, like a reed in the wind, had bowed to Elvis's every wish. If he wanted her to wear darker eye makeup, she did. He liked sexy clothes and spiked heels, so she shopped to please him. She learned the hard way that she was not to talk back. When angry, Elvis would address her as "woman," often following it with an assertion of his authority.

During the four years that they lived together, Elvis often stayed in Hollywood, starring in movies, having affairs with his leading ladies, and generally living a bachelor's life with the guys. Under orders, Priscilla stayed at home. Elvis believed, like many men, in the double standard. It was fine for him to have affairs; after all, he wasn't married to Priscilla—and he was a man! From Priscilla, absolute loyalty was not only expected, it was demanded. And there were plenty of people at Graceland who would let Elvis know if his little girl was up to something.

With all of these difficulties, this was the only life that Priscilla had known from the moment she moved into Graceland. And she remained steadfast in her belief that marriage and a family would be hers someday. Elvis just needed his freedom now. If his behavior seems immature and disrespectful of Priscilla, it was. The problem that Elvis always had, not only with her but with all of his close relationships, was that he could get away with anything. As the surviving son, he had always been his mother's darling. By his late teens he had assumed the role of the family breadwinner, and shortly afterward he became the object of adoration and love from the whole world. These conditions almost by necessity breed selfish and excessive behavior.

Treated like a king by those around him, Elvis behaved as one with royal privilege. If his behavior to Priscilla was mean and hurtful one moment, the next moment he would lavish expensive gifts upon her, expressing his undying love and behaving like a vulnerable little boy.

By 1966, four years had passed since Priscilla had moved to Graceland. Elvis had assured Captain Beaulieu that he would eventually "do right" by his daughter when the time came. To Captain Beaulieu, four years was plenty of time. He had had enough of Elvis's procrastination and demanded to know Elvis's intentions.

Elvis was clearly not ready to marry, but he was torn by his commitment to Priscilla's father. The conflict he felt over this situation added to other big problems: the boredom and disgust he felt for the movies he was starring in. All of this began to affect his behavior.

He turned first to spiritualism. Under the guidance of his mystically inclined hairdresser, Larry Geller, Elvis devoured books on all of the world's religions and paths to enlighten-

On May 1, 1967, Elvis married Priscilla
Beaulieu in Las Vegas. He had first met
her while he was stationed in Germany in
1959. She was fourteen when they met.

ment. Also during this time, Elvis and Priscilla experimented with street drugs for the first time, taking LSD and smoking marijuana. Elvis was using prescription medicines even more frequently now, uppers for energy and to lose weight, and sleeping pills and tranquilizers to come down.

Elvis appeared to be ambivalent about his commitment to Priscilla, and his interest in spiritual matters was but another way of dealing with his conflict. Elvis reassured the captain that he would marry Priscilla—in time. Meanwhile, he found a new pastime: ranching. Elvis went on a wild spree in which he spent over a million dollars to buy a ranch near Graceland, outfitting it with horses, equipment, and pickup trucks for each of the guys and their wives.

To the alarm of the director on his next movie, *Clambake*, he had also gone on an eating spree. His weight ballooned up to over 200 pounds (91 kg). One night before he was to report to the set, he tripped over a TV wire in the middle of the night, raising a lump on his head. The doctors were called and found that he had suffered a concussion. At great cost to the studio, the filming had to be delayed. The Colonel, panicked at the condition of his boy, swiftly ousted the spiritualist, the books, and Elvis's excuses. Marriage, the Colonel said, would straighten him out. Taking his mentor's advice as always, Elvis finally set the date for the wedding.

On May 1, 1967, Elvis and Priscilla were married in Las Vegas. Elvis was thirty-two, Priscilla, twenty-one. Joe Esposito and Marty Lacker were the only members of the Memphis Mafia on hand to witness the ceremony. The Colonel and Priscilla had agreed that Elvis had been paying too many salaries and had kept his mind away from work for too long.

At the ceremony in the Aladdin Hotel, Elvis looked shaky. During the press conference after the ceremony, he told the reporters, "I'm a little bit nervous, you know. There's no way out of it. We appear calm, but Ed Sullivan didn't scare me this much."

Elvis and Priscilla moved into a wealthy new development in Los Angeles, Trousdale Estates. Priscilla went to work decorating their new home. Elvis went back to work on the set of *Clambake*, his twenty-fifth movie. Though not much was changing in his career, Elvis had begun a move back to his musical roots. In March he released a gospel album entitled *How Great Thou Art*, a record that would win Elvis his only Grammy Award. Within a month of the wedding, Priscilla had become pregnant. On February 1, 1968, Lisa Marie Presley was born and Elvis once again found the stability of a family.

STARTING OVER

By 1968, Elvis's claim to the title of the King of rock and roll had slipped away. Pop music had changed. Groups like the Doors, the Grateful Dead, as well as Janis Joplin and the Jefferson Airplane, dominated the imagination of American youth. Rock music turned political, and angry. The British influence continued with the Who and the Rolling Stones, groups who revitalized the rock and roll that Elvis had practically invented by returning to its early sources.

Meanwhile, Elvis's movie sound tracks barely reached *Billboard*'s Top 100. Attendance at the films fell off. He was bored with his career, and he continued to spend money frantically. Elvis, who had it all, was profoundly unhappy. The Colonel, not a dull-witted man by any stretch of the imagination, sensed that change—and perhaps a challenge—would be necessary.

Colonel Parker decided that Elvis would do a TV special, his first one ever. The Colonel wanted a Christmas Show and contacted NBC. They were delighted with the idea, but the

Colonel immediately locked horns with a young producer who had his own ideas about Elvis's return to performing.

Steve Binder had been moved by Elvis's early music and wanted to present the Hillbilly Cat as he had first appeared on the scene: raw, vital, even a little dangerous. He wanted America to get a good look at the legend. In other words, he wanted Elvis to play *live*, in front of an audience while he filmed it. The Colonel was opposed to all of this.

A nice safe Christmas program, that's what the Colonel had in mind. After all, the show's sponsor was the Singer Sewing Machine Company. To the Colonel, a Christmas special meant Elvis would sing fifteen or twenty Yuletide carols, introduce a few guests, and wave "Happy Holidays" to the nation.

On December 3, 1968, it was clear from the show's opening just who had prevailed. Dressed in black leather from neck to toe, a slimmed down, ready-to-rock Elvis filled the TV screen. To get the message across, the show opened with "Trouble Man," a song that asks this question: "Lookin' for trouble? Then look in my face."

One of Elvis's bodyguards, Lamar Fike, aptly described his boss's appearance that night: "Thin as a rake and handsomer than ten movie stars." For most of America, Elvis was reborn that night. He looked and sounded better than they had remembered.

For part of the show, he appeared onstage with only a few of his old musician friends, surrounded on three sides by the audience. When he took the mike for "Hound Dog," his hand trembled with fear. His anxiety had been almost overwhelming. "What if they laugh at me?" he had asked one of the producers just days before the taping.

Elvis hadn't performed in front of a live audience for eight years, and he was afraid they would think of him as a dinosaur, a relic. Many of the songs he sang that night were his

early hits, but, after his nervousness subsided, America witnessed what came close to a reincarnation. The songs were the same, but the singer was a different man. His voice had mellowed, his stagecraft appeared more confident. Elvis performed at the peak of his powers, and the audience loved every minute. When he ran off the stage after taping the live segments, he was jubilant. In his boyish manner he exulted, "They still like me."

This program, now referred to among Elvis's fans as the "comeback special," turned his faltering career around. The reviews this time were unanimous in their praise. The stodgy *New York Times*, which had pilloried him time and again during his rise to stardom, joined in, calling Elvis "charismatic."

Elvis's records began to sell briskly again, and the closing song to the special, "If I Can Dream," became his first big single in years. More important, though, the renewed contact with his fans sent a jolt of energy through him. Now, Elvis knew, he had to be out in front of an audience again.

CONQUERING VEGAS

The return to Las Vegas wasn't Elvis's idea. The Colonel had worked out a deal which gave them $100,000 a week to headline at the biggest, splashiest hotel that Vegas had ever

*Elvis's 1968 comeback performance.
Dressed in black leather from head
to toe, he created a sensation.
Bodyguard Lamar Fike described him
as "thin as a rake and handsomer
than ten movie stars." And his voice
was better than ever.*

seen. The International Hotel, with fifteen hundred rooms, was the tallest building in Nevada, and the grandest thing on the already glamorous Strip. The Showroom Internationale, the nightclub where Elvis was to perform, contained two thousand seats and a monstrous stage.

The whole idea intimidated him. Even Barbra Streisand, then at the peak of her performing career, couldn't keep this room filled during her engagement. To bolster his confidence, Elvis enlisted the aid of the musicians who had accompanied him on the Singer special, a bunch of crack Memphis session players. These guys had come up with the Memphis sound, a gritty mix of rock and r&b that put the sizzle into his TV program. Perhaps they would recreate that feat in Las Vegas.

Elvis walked out onto the stage on July 31, 1969, without an introduction, just the way he started his shows in 1954. About to begin the first song, he stood frozen in his tracks at the thunderous roar of the audience. When the audience recognized the figure, they stood as one and hit him in the face with a roar of approval that paralyzed him. When the swell subsided, he struck the trademark pose of his early years, microphone front and center, legs popping like he couldn't wait to begin. And then he let loose.

"We l l l l . . . It's one for the money . . . two for the show . . . three to get ready, now go cat, go . . ." "Blue Suede Shoes," a number everyone in the audience knew, started the show off with a high-energy crackle that didn't subside for an hour. Elvis gave them all the old hits, adding new words here and there, as if to say to the crowd, "I know these may be silly old songs, but you loved them, and I know you want to hear them again." He laughed at himself, at his old macho image, at his new movie image. Elvis let down the guard, and the audience loved it.

Then he went into his new songs, recorded only six months ago with a new band in a new studio. "In the Ghet-

News reporters interviewed the King on his
triumphant return to Las Vegas in 1969.
He told them, "I'm really glad to be back
in front of a live audience."

to," Elvis told the audience humbly, "has been a big seller for me. . . . Something I really needed." "Suspicious Minds," his first number-one single since 1962, received the deluxe Las Vegas treatment. Full orchestra and slam-bam choreography. Elvis had designed his new stage moves, based on the martial arts and karate, which he had been studying for years. It was a spectacular display, and the audience responded with another standing ovation, as if to say, we not only love the Elvis we remember, we are ready to love him now.

The King of rock and roll had returned to conquer the city that had scorned him once before. Las Vegas hadn't changed much. It was still a middle-class, middle-aged city. But this audience had fifteen years of memories; they had heard Elvis when they were teenagers, and he brought to life and then some the days when rock and roll was vital and a little risky.

A band of the most respected rock critics, flown out for this performance by the crafty old Colonel, raised their voices in praise. *Rolling Stone* said, "Elvis was supernatural, his own resurrection. . . ." The month-long engagement closed out in August 1969, having attracted 101,000 customers, a Las Vegas record that would go unequaled for some time. He would return to the hotel in February for another extended engagement, a twice-a-year routine that would continue for the next seven years.

THE FINAL YEARS

Once Elvis had been assured that his fans still loved him, he longed to get back on the road. He returned to Las Vegas only five months later for another two months of sellout shows. Then came six performances at the huge Houston Astrodome and a short tour of six cities in six days in the fall.

This pattern of work endured for the next seven years. One thousand and ninety-four concerts in 130 cities. Twice a year to Las Vegas for monthlong gigs, followed by whirlwind trips across the American heartland. During this time, Elvis's use of prescription drugs increased madly—amphetamines to keep him up and barbiturates to bring him to rest. He turned into a nocturnal creature with habits and rituals as strange as those of Howard Hughes.

To keep the King comfortable on tour, his men prepared all the hotel rooms in advance. Aluminum foil taped over the windows prevented daylight from disturbing his sleep. The air conditioning was turned down so low that most people would have been very uncomfortable. Night was day, and daytime was for sleeping. During these years of touring, Elvis, the performer, played before millions of people, yet he isolated himself from his public by his own choice. He surrounded himself only with people that he knew and trusted.

Almost all of these friends were "on the payroll," which means that they depended upon Elvis for their livelihood. Though they had families of their own, they were first and foremost the King's men. Elvis preferred to be called the Boss, and he demanded loyalty from the guys. If he wanted to shoot rifles and machine guns in the middle of the night, he expected to have company. They learned karate and racquetball with him. If he turned to a yogurt diet to lose weight, they all ate yogurt. They shared the drugs and the women, but they could not share Elvis's increasing despair.

Beginning with his triumph at Las Vegas, and continuing through the years of relentless touring, Elvis saw less and less of Priscilla and Lisa Marie. He could not give up his bachelor's life-style or the company of the guys. In fact, there was a strict rule, "No wives on the road," which meant that the wives were not around much of the time.

Priscilla was used to being alone—at Graceland, she

hardly saw Elvis when he worked in Hollywood—but something was different now. "It was the day Elvis suggested I come to Las Vegas less often that I became really upset and suspicious," she wrote in her book, *Elvis and Me*. She was well aware of the life-style of musicians on the road, but she did not want it for herself or for Lisa Marie. Though Elvis had encouraged her to take sleeping pills with him when she was just a teenager, drugs had little appeal for Priscilla, then and now. She wanted a proper home and a proper husband, and it gradually dawned on her that this was not possible with a man like Elvis Presley.

He had conquered Las Vegas. He had conquered all of America with his comeback. He had met the challenge of re-creating himself, but soon he began to get bored repeating his performances so many times in a year.

In 1969, the infamous Charles Manson murders of actress Sharon Tate and her friends held the headlines for weeks. The murders deeply disturbed Elvis—they had occurred only miles from his California home. In the public eye once again, he began to receive death threats. Elvis felt exposed and vulnerable and he hated to feel that way. From this year on, Elvis began a preoccupation with guns that reached paranoid proportions.

Priscilla remembered his condition at the time: "Bored and restless, he increased his dependence on chemicals. He thought speed helped him escape from destructive thinking, when in reality it gave him false confidence and unnatural aggressiveness. He started losing perspective on himself and others. To me he became increasingly unreachable."

Priscilla decided to leave Elvis. She left him for a man he had introduced to her, karate instructor Mike Stone. When he tried and failed to get her back, Elvis became inconsolable. During this time his behavior became even more bizarre and erratic. He tried to have Stone killed by Mafia hitmen. Those who knew him well say that it was Priscilla's decision to go through with a divorce that took the spirit out of Elvis.

One of the most worshiped men in the history of show business decided to deal with his disappointment by throwing himself into his work. In 1973, the year that they were divorced, Elvis continued his breakneck pace of performing with two months in Las Vegas and multi-city tours in April and June. A benefit performance from Honolulu was broadcast via satellite to over one billion viewers in forty countries.

Although he refined and tinkered with his touring act, it remained the same old Las Vegas show. The sameness of it bored him, so he dressed it up with elaborate costumes and stage productions. With his beaded, bejeweled jumpsuits and flowing capes, Elvis adopted the look of a fantasy king or even a god, certainly a comic book hero. He entered the stage to the majestic opening notes of "Also Sprach Zara-thustra," Richard Strauss's composition (it was used in the movie *2001: A Space Odyssey*). To his most frantic female subjects, he dispensed scarves by the dozens during every show. He behaved like a king amid his adoring public.

Elvis's road show became, as other writers have pointed out, a ritual that was played out every year to millions of faithful. Despite his dissatisfaction, Elvis continued to perform the ritual, just as he continued to act in movies that he hated. Why he did so is another question that can't be answered simply. Elvis had always seen performing as a "job," and it was the only job he knew how to do.

Though he changed the course of popular culture, Elvis saw himself primarily as an entertainer. He felt he shared more in common with Dean Martin and Frank Sinatra than with the Beatles. He also did it because he was told to do it. The Colonel still called the shots when it came to business.

He did it for the money, too, although he had never had any idea of the value of money. More likely, he did it so he wouldn't have to worry about money.

In the last years of his life, Elvis developed the
ritual of tossing scarves to his fans to keep as souvenirs
of his performance. For this concert before 13,500
people in Providence, Rhode Island, he dressed in
a white jumpsuit covered with gold brocade.

He did it also because it needed to be done. After rising to the challenge of rekindling his career, and finding the world still loved him and his music, perhaps there was nothing left for him to do but to continually perform this ritual.

During the last few years of his life, Elvis replayed a pattern that he established in 1970. First Vegas, then the tours, and finally a return to Memphis. At Graceland, he would indulge himself—eat whatever he wanted, do whatever he wanted. His weight often ballooned up to 230 pounds (104 kg) on a diet of southern-fried foods. Then, he would starve himself for three weeks before the next performance. He took diet pills to help him trim down, and sleeping pills to relax.

From his twenties on, Elvis had turned to prescription medicines to change his moods. He could afford plenty of doctors and pharmacists who would prescribe whatever he wanted. Somehow, Elvis refused to believe that he had become addicted—(perhaps because the pills were prescribed by doctors)—or that these medications were dangerous.

He despised junkies—those pathetic devils who were hooked on street drugs like heroin and cocaine—and for a time volunteered his (and the guys') services to the Memphis police department to bring a few of them to justice.

A doctor's prescription gave him the license to lose his soul to chemical dependency. To Elvis, the drugs he took weren't dope, but medicine dispensed by authority figures dressed in white. He really believed it. He also believed that his vast knowledge of drugs would protect him from their harmful effects. These beliefs cost Elvis his life.

THE END

The King was preparing for another tour on August 15, 1977. Though he had fasted for two days, he was still grossly overweight at 255 pounds (116 kg). He was upset at himself for this and for other reasons as well. His former bodyguards had written a book that was about to be published. *Elvis: What Happened?* revealed his drug habits, his attraction to guns, his eating binges, his bizarre behavior. The publication of these secrets by his once trusted bodyguards deeply offended his sense of loyalty and sent him into a deeper depression.

It was a night like many other nights at Graceland. Elvis had gone to the dentist to have a filling repaired before he hit the road. He popped his amphetamines. He played racquetball deep into the evening. When he wanted to sleep, he found himself unable to. In the early morning, he took a book, *The Scientific Search for the Face of Jesus,* into his large bathroom and reading room.

His girlfriend, Ginger Alden, warned him not to fall asleep in there, as he had many times before when the sleeping pills took over. He replied, "Okay, I won't," his last words.

The next day, Ginger found Elvis at about one o'clock in the afternoon, crumpled on the floor and cold to the touch. He was rushed to Baptist Hospital, where despite the doctor's attempts at resuscitation, he was pronounced dead. The autopsy, the subject of continuing controversy, revealed that he had ten different drugs, in significant quantities, in his body when his heart stopped.

The news spread, and within hours of Elvis Presley's death, mourners began to gather at Graceland's gates. Their numbers would swell to the thousands as the news spread through the land. The King was dead. Heads of state from twenty different countries formally mourned Elvis's passing. The networks covered the funeral live, devoting nearly as much attention to it as they would to a presidential assassination. Practically every newspaper in America saluted Elvis in their editorial columns.

From the White House, President Jimmy Carter tried to express the nation's grief.

"Elvis Presley's death deprives our country of a part of itself. He was unique, and irreplaceable. More than twenty years ago, he burst upon the scene with an impact that was unprecedented and will probably never be equaled. His music and his personality, fusing the styles of white country and black rhythm-and-blues, permanently changed the face of American popular culture. His following was immense and he was a symbol to people the world over, of the vitality, the rebelliousness, and good humor of his country."

GETTING TO KNOW ELVIS

FOR FURTHER READING

A list of all the published material on Elvis Presley would easily take up a book this size. What follows is a very selective reading list. Some of these books are biographies; others discuss Elvis as one of the early figures of rock and roll. Several have detailed bibliographies and discographies.

Goldman, Albert. *Elvis.* New York: McGraw-Hill, 1981.

The author conducted six hundred interviews during the course of writing this book. Much of it focuses on Elvis's dark side—the drugs, the infidelities, the obsession with firearms. Goldman's *Elvis* is not only well researched, but well written, and much of it is fascinating. In the end, though, the reader is left with the impression that the author is repelled not only by Elvis, but by the South and by rock and roll music.

Hopkins, Jerry. *Elvis.* New York: Simon & Schuster, 1971.
_____. *Elvis: The Final Years.* New York: St. Martin's Press, 1980.

These books were written with the cooperation of Colonel Tom Parker and many other important figures in Elvis's life. Therefore, most of the facts are accurate. Hopkins is also a lively writer, and the books are enjoyable.

Marcus, Greil. *Mystery Train: Images of America in Rock 'n' Roll Music.* New York: Dutton, 1975.

The subtitle to this book explains what the author has successfully set out to explore. Elvis's life and his impact on American popular culture are discussed in the brilliant 15,000-word closing section to *Mystery Train.* This rich, complicated tribute represents the earliest serious discussion of Elvis and forms the bedrock for much of the analysis that followed.

Marsh, Dave. *Elvis.* New York: Rolling Stone Press/Times Books, 1982.

A loving presentation of Elvis's life and musical career. The writing, mostly an analysis of Elvis as a mythic American figure, is superb and passionate. The photographs are lovingly reproduced and the whole package is a tribute to Elvis and to rock and roll.

Presley, Priscilla Beaulieu, with Harmon, Sandra. *Elvis and Me.* New York: Putnam, 1985.

Priscilla's side of the story naturally reveals more about her than about Elvis. Priscilla's book does, however, shed a little more light on their complex relationship, but most of all helps readers to understand the resilient and patient fourteen-year-old girl who captured Elvis's heart.

West, Red: West, Sonny; Hebler, Dave; as told to Steve Dunleavy. *Elvis: What Happened?* New York: Ballantine Books, 1977.

The book that disturbed Elvis during his final days came from three of his longtime buddies and bodyguards in the Memphis Mafia. They told what they knew about Elvis's personal life to a New York newspaper reporter who turned it into the definitive scandal book. The book was designed to make money for men who had worked for Elvis for years and who were dismissed from the Presley payroll. Some of Red West's recollections about Elvis as a high school kid, however, are touching and revealing.

Worth, Fred L., and Tamerius, Steve D. *All About Elvis.* New York: Bantam Books, 1981.

An encyclopedia of fascinating information, facts, and trivia, not only about Elvis but about many of the people who touched his life. This is not a biography or an analysis of Elvis, but rather a compendium of information that is fun to have alongside a biography.

LISTENING LIST

As an introduction to Elvis for a new generation of listeners, perhaps the most accessible record is RCA's collection entitled *Rocker*, which was released in 1984. This record contains the classics "Blue Suede Shoes," "Jailhouse Rock," "Hound Dog," and "Shake, Rattle and Roll," among others that were all recorded in a sixteen-month period during 1956 and 1957.

Elvis's love for gospel music never left him. Sacred music always strengthened and reassured him, and he often gathered other musicians and singers around the piano before he would perform or record. He recorded several albums of religious music, but perhaps the best one is *How Great Thou Art*, which won a Grammy Award in the best sacred performance category.

Elvis: The Sun Sessions, an LP of the singles recorded in the Sun Studio between July 1954 and November 1955, released by RCA Records in 1976. This record contains the early rockabilly recordings Elvis made for Sam Phillips in Memphis; in other words, the songs that all the fuss was about.

Elvis Country, released in 1971, contains standard country numbers, some old ("Make the World Go Away"), some new (Kris Kristofferson's "Help Me Make It Through the Night"), as well as a version of Jerry Lee Lewis's rock classic, "Whole Lotta Shakin' Goin' On."

For a selection of his best-selling records, listen to any of the six albums in RCA's collection entitled *Elvis' Gold Records*. The later volumes will contain some of his better material from his later years.

A complete list of Elvis's RCA recordings can be obtained by writing to RCA Records, 1133 Avenue of the Americas, New York, NY 10036, or look in the discography sections of the books listed above.

FILMS

Most of Elvis's movies are now available on videotape. A few are definitely worth watching. *Jailhouse Rock*, released in 1957, contains the great dance number set to the title song. *Viva Las Vegas!*, a 1964 film in which Elvis starred with Ann-Margret is perhaps the best of the 1960s movies, maybe because the leading lady is for once fitting competition for Elvis.

Also available on videotape are some fine examples of Elvis performing. The 1968 NBC-TV special, which is titled "Elvis," shows him looking his fittest and singing with passion. His energy on this program—before a live audience—came from his doubts that his audience would still be there after an eight-year absence from performing. Much of the show will seem old-fashioned compared to music videos, but

A scene from the movie,
Jailhouse Rock.

the part to watch is Elvis performing on a small stage, sur-rounded by some of the musicians that were with him from his early days.

Elvis on Tour, a theatrical film released in 1972, won a Golden Globe award in the best documentary category. This film captures Elvis as the King of the concert hall, the master of a massive Vegas stage show that he took on the road with little change until he died. Although the movie doesn't reveal much of Elvis (he's always behind dark glasses, always kid-ding and always singing), it is worth watching for the spec-tacle.

INDEX

ABOUT THE AUTHOR

Robert Love is a senior editor at *Rolling Stone* magazine. A former rock musician and guitar instructor, he recorded his first and only "demo" record at the age of fourteen at the Dynamic Sound studio, in Hicksville, New York. His love of rock and roll music and journalism led to a career that combines both.

Mr. Love lives in New York City, and has written articles for *New York* magazine, *Esquire*, and *Guitar Player*. This is his first book for Franklin Watts.